INDIAN PATRIOTS Of The GREAT WEST

 A TARGET BOOK

INDIAN PATRIOTS
Of The
GREAT WEST

Edited, with commentary by Bennett Wayne

GARRARD PUBLISHING COMPANY
CHAMPAIGN, ILLINOIS

Library of Congress Cataloging in Publication Data

Wayne, Bennett.
   Indian patriots of the Great West.

   (Target)
   SUMMARY: Brief biographies of four Indian
chiefs: Sitting Bull, Crazy Horse, Chief Joseph,
and Quanah Parker.
   1. Indians of North America—The West—
Biography—Juvenile literature. [1. Indians of
North America—The West—Biography]. I. Title.
E78.W5W37   970.4'8 [B] [920]   73–17110
ISBN 0–8116–4906–7

Acknowledgments:

The words of Sitting Bull, Crazy Horse, Quanah Parker,
and Chief Joseph are from the following sources:
Page 50: 1. Johnson, W.F. *Life of Sitting Bull and
            History of the Indian War of 1890-1891.*
            Edgewood Publishing Company, 1891, Pp. 201-202.
         2. Wheeler, Homer W. *Buffalo Days.* Indianapolis,
            Bobbs-Merrill Company, 1925, P. 253.
Page 86: 1. McLuhan, T.C. *Touch the Earth.* New York,
            Outerbridge & Dienstfrey, 1971, P. 67.
         2. U.S. Commissioner of Indian Affairs,
            Annual Report, 1875, P. 188.
Page 122:   Tilghman, Zoe A. *Quanah: The Eagle of the
            Comanches.* Oklahoma City, Harlow Publishing
            Company, 1938, Pp. 62, 127.
Page 160: 1. Brown, Dee. *Bury My Heart at Wounded Knee.*
            New York, Holt, Rinehart and Winston, Inc.,
            1970, P. 321.
         2. Howard, Helen Addison. *War Chief Joseph.*
            The Caxton Printers, 1941, P. 84.

Contents

The Patriot Chiefs

When these Plains Indians rode to the hunt, the buffalo were so many that they could not be counted. Sioux and Blackfoot, Cheyenne and Comanche rode swiftly across the prairie in search of the great, shaggy, life-giving beasts. Yet, within a generation, the buffalo were gone, and the glory days of the Indians were over. They had vanished before the white man, one Indian chief wrote, "as snow before the summer sun." How did it happen?

At first only a few white men had seen the West. But soon the few became many. Under the protection of the army, miners, buffalo hunters, and settlers poured onto Indian lands. Solemn treaties became worthless pieces of paper. With their lands overrun and the buffalo fast disappearing, the Indians lashed out in anger at the intruders. The army was quick to fight back, and terrible deeds on one side resulted in terrible deeds on the other. Soon there was open warfare on the plains.

There was never much doubt about the outcome. The Indians could not long withstand the large numbers of well-equipped soldiers who were sent to the Great Plains after the Civil War. And they could not continue to live in freedom on the prairie after hunters had destroyed the herds of wild buffalo. By 1889 the last battle had been fought, the buffalo were gone, and the remaining Plains Indians were living on reservations.

How it all happened is told here in the life stories of four great Indian chiefs of western tribes: Sitting Bull and Crazy Horse of the Sioux, Quanah Parker of the Comanches, and Chief Joseph of the Nez Perces. Patriots all, they fought desperately for the right of their people to live freely in the lands of their ancestors—and for a way of life that was doomed when the very first white man ventured West.

Sitting Bull

Great Sioux Chief

by LaVere Anderson

Neither Grandfather's words nor well-armed troops could stop the great Sioux leader from fighting for his people's rights. His Sioux warriors wiped out Long Hair Custer's forces in the last great battle at the Little Bighorn, but it proved to be, as Sitting Bull predicted, "too big a victory."

9

1. Grizzly Bear!

The Sioux Indian boy lay asleep under a cottonwood tree on the bank of the Grand River. He was alone and far from his village. All morning he had hunted with bow and arrow through the summer woods, but he had not seen one rabbit or squirrel. At last, hot and tired, he had lain down to rest. His eyes grew heavy. He fell asleep.

The boy's name was Slow. Someday when he was older and had done brave deeds his father would give him another name. Now he was twelve, and he was called Slow because he took time to think before he acted. A boy needed to think carefully and to be on his guard in the Dakota country in 1843. In such a wild land there were many dangers.

Slow awoke with a start. Overhead he heard a tapping.

He looked up and saw a yellow bird sitting on a branch of the cottonwood tree. It was a little yellowhammer, and it tapped the branch sharply with its beak. *Tap-tap! Tap-tap!*

"Your noise awoke me," Slow scolded the bird.

While he lay there he heard another noise. Something was crashing through the woods. Suddenly from out of the trees came a great brown grizzly bear.

The frightened boy lay still, not knowing what to do, for grizzlies were fierce beasts. Even the bravest warriors were afraid of them. Slow knew it was no use to fight. His small arrows were not made to go through a grizzly's thick fur and tough layers of fat.

It was no use to run. A grizzly could run faster than a grown man. It was no use to jump into the river. A grizzly could swim. It was no use to climb the cottonwood. A grizzly could climb any tree that would hold its weight.

No, Slow thought, it was no use to do anything except lie still. Sometimes a grizzly would not attack if one played dead.

On came the bear, right up to the boy, who hardly dared breathe. The bear nosed Slow's moccasins. It sniffed his bare legs. Slow could feel the beast's rough shaggy hair brushing his body, and he could hear its huffing growls.

Although he could not see the bear, Slow knew how fearsome it looked. Its huge paws were strong enough to crush a horse's skull with one blow. Its big yellow teeth could bite through solid bone. Its claws were as long and sharp as arrowheads.

Slow felt the grizzly's hot breath on his face. Then as noisily as it had come, the bear left. Slow opened one eye a little and watched it go, swinging its head from side to side as it tried to catch a scent on the air. He lay still until he could no longer hear it crashing through the dark woods.

At last he sat up. The yellow bird looked down from its branch, and Slow looked back. He knew that the bird had saved his life by waking him with its tapping. Suddenly he felt a great love for the tiny creature.

"Pretty yellow bird, I will never forget you," he said softly. "All my life I will be a friend to all Bird People because of you."

Then the boy picked up his bow and arrows and started for the circle of tepees that made up his village. He would have exciting news to tell about the grizzly, and about his new friends the Bird People.

2. Dakota Boy

On the way home Slow saw a red squirrel. He shot it with one arrow. Now he had meat to take to his mother.

Hunting was not a sport to the young Sioux. It was important work. All the meat a boy could find was welcome in the Sioux camp. It tasted good to the hungry Indians—porcupine, beaver, raccoon, prairie dog, muskrat, even skunk. Sometimes Slow caught a fish in the river on a bone hook baited with grasshoppers. Sometimes he found a big turtle.

The real name of the Sioux people was the Dakota Nation. Many of them lived in what is now South Dakota and Nebraska. The nation was divided into branches. One of these branches was called the Hunkpapa Sioux. Slow was a Hunkpapa.

Slow lived a life of great freedom. In 1843, when he was twelve, there were not many white men in Sioux country. The plains and forests were Slow's playground. All the rivers were his swimming pools.

When he reached the village, Slow gave the squirrel to his mother, Mixed Day. Quickly she cleaned it and dropped the meat into a buffalo paunch to cook. A paunch was the tough skin of a buffalo's stomach. Filled with water and held up by four strong sticks, it made a good soup pot.

Mixed Day put wild potatoes and onions and prairie turnips into the pot with the meat. She kept the soup boiling by dropping hot stones into the paunch.

Slow's two sisters and their friends returned from picking wild plums. Slow told about the grizzly. Then he went to look for his father, Jumping Bull.

A Sioux village on the Great Plains

It was a happy, peaceful village through which Slow walked. The blue smoke of evening cooking fires rose above the buffalo-hide tepees. There was a good smell of roasting buffalo meat. A young man was playing his flute made of bird-wing bone, and the soft music sounded as sweet as a dove's call.

It was a busy village, too. Some boys wrestled while others raced their ponies. Young girls played with buckskin dolls and older girls sat sewing deerskin clothing. Women worked at the cooking fires, and tiny children played nearby. Nobody stopped a child who got too close to the blaze.

"One must learn from the bite of the fire to let it alone," the adults said. The Sioux believed that children should learn everything from experience.

Slow found his father sitting with other men planning a buffalo hunt.

Like all Plains Indians, the Sioux depended on the buffalo for food and other needs. They followed the buffalo herds and moved their villages when the herds moved. Buffalo are ugly beasts—dark and shaggy, with big humps on their backs and red-rimmed eyes—but to the Indians they were known as "the givers of life." They gave meat and tallow, warm hides for blankets and tepees, bones for tools, hair for rope, horns for spoons, and many other useful things.

When the men had finished talking, Slow told Jumping Bull about the grizzly.

"You acted wisely, my son," his father said. All the men nodded. "Slow thinks before he acts," they agreed.

That night Slow sat with other children at the evening campfire. They listened to their elders tell hero tales of Sioux history—tales of great deeds that the nation had done in the past. The council fire was like a schoolroom for the children. There they learned how to be good Sioux.

Slow liked to hear the stories. He crowded close

to listen. He was proud to be a Hunkpapa, a mighty branch of the greatest Indian nation. Already he had learned from the stories that there were four important things a Hunkpapa must be.

He must be brave. He must be strong in bearing pain and trouble. He must be generous. He must be wise. These were the four Sioux virtues.

"I can teach myself to be brave and to bear pain," Slow thought. "I can make myself be generous. But to be wise—that is harder."

Then he remembered his father's words about the grizzly. "You acted wisely, my son," he had said.

A smile broke over the boy's face. "Perhaps I can grow up to be wise, too!" he thought.

Overhead, a round yellow moon shone down on the Sioux village. It lighted the smiling face of the boy, who did not know he would grow up to be the wisest man of all his people.

3. Counting "Coup"

The Hunkpapa Sioux were going on the warpath. Slow watched the braves put on war paint made from colored earths, charcoal, and tallow. He wanted to go with the war party, but everyone thought him just a boy. Although he was fourteen now, he was small for his age.

Sadly he watched his father get ready to leave. Jumping Bull was a great warrior. He wore a breech clout and moccasins. He carried weapons and a shield. As Jumping Bull rode away, Mixed Day stood by the tepee and sang the brave heart song for him.

"I am strong, and I have a fast pony," Slow told himself. "I would not shame my father in battle." He thought of a plan.

That evening the Sioux warriors camped beside a stream. At daylight they were going to attack their old enemies, the Crows. The Crow Indians were neighbors of the Sioux. Often the Crows and the Sioux fought because of disputes over hunting grounds.

Stars were shining brightly when Slow rode into camp. He had known where the war party would stop, and his pony was very fast. It had not been hard to catch up. Slow was painted yellow from head to foot. His gray pony was colored red. The pair was ready for battle.

"We are ready to fight," Slow told his surprised father.

Many Hunkpapas laughed. Good-Voiced-Elk, the leader, said, "Fourteen winters and the boy thinks he is a warrior! Let him go back and wait with the women and children."

Jumping Bull looked troubled. He feared for his only son's safety, yet he knew that it would shame the boy to send him home now. At last he said, "My son will ride with us."

He gave Slow a coup stick—a long stick with a feather tied on the end. When a warrior touched an enemy with such a stick, it was called "counting coup." To count coup was as brave an act as to kill an enemy. Every warrior wanted to count many coups to prove his courage.

At dawn the war party set out. In a short while they spied a party of Crows coming toward them across the plains. *"Hopo! Hopo!"* shouted Good-Voiced-Elk. "Let's go! Let's go!"

The Sioux, a people known for their bravery in warfare, battle with a neighboring band of Indians.

But the Crows turned and raced away. They thought the Sioux war party was much larger than their own. The Sioux chased them.

Slow leaned low on his pony's neck. "*Hopo!*" he cried into its ear. Swift as the wind, the little pony raced ahead and took the lead.

Soon Slow caught up with a Crow brave. Slow's father had given him no lance or war arrows. His only weapon was the coup stick, but it was enough. He meant to be the first to count coup.

Straight for the enemy went boy and pony. Quickly the Crow brave fitted an arrow to his bow. Before he could shoot, Slow was upon him. Slow hit out with his stick. The blow knocked the Crow off balance. He fell from his horse.

"*On-hey!* I, Slow, have conquered him!" shouted the excited boy as other Sioux rode up to him.

The battle was over quickly, for the Sioux could not catch many of the fleeing Crow. Slow was the hero. Without weapons he had charged the enemy, and he had been the first to count coup.

When they returned to their village, Jumping Bull put Slow on his own big bay horse. Then the father led the horse through the village and called proudly to the people: "My son has struck the enemy! He is brave! I name him Sitting Bull!"

The boy gasped in delight. Sitting Bull! It was an

honor name like his father's! It came from the Buffalo God, who was one of the greatest of Indian gods.

The people were pleased. "*Hau!*" they cried. "Yes! He is Sitting Bull!"

That night the village held a victory dance. Drums beat. Happy voices sang the victory song. Around the fire the warriors leaped and whirled in a wild victory dance. Sitting Bull danced with them, for he had helped win that victory.

4. Sitting Bull Adopts a Brother

The years passed swiftly. Sitting Bull grew tall, with broad shoulders and a deep chest. He rode on many warpaths and counted many coups. Sitting Bull became a member of the Hunkpapa warrior society. These young men were called the Strong Hearts because each had proved himself in battle.

Soon Sitting Bull was made chief of the Strong Hearts. "We are Sitting Bull's men!" his warriors would shout as they were led into battle. That war cry struck terror in the hearts of the enemy.

One icy winter day Sitting Bull's warriors attacked the village of an enemy tribe, the Assiniboines of Montana. Some Assiniboines were killed, and some escaped. Only one Indian was left—an eleven-year-old boy whose parents lay dead in the snow. He faced the Hunkpapas bravely with his small bow and a single arrow. He was ready to fight alone.

One by one the Hunkpapas rode up and touched him with their coup sticks. He did not shrink away although he knew that when the last had counted coup, he would be killed. It was the custom. His own people would have done the same to a Sioux.

Sitting Bull rode up. The boy saw something in this warrior's face he had not seen in the others. Hope stirred in the boy's eyes. He spoke two words: "Big brother."

Those words went straight to Sitting Bull's heart. He had never had a brother. Instantly he moved his pony in front of the boy, like a shield. "This boy must live!" Sitting Bull shouted. "He is too brave to die!"

Fierce-looking No-Neck spoke in a loud voice: "He is our enemy. He will grow up and take revenge on us for his parents. He will kill our people and then laugh at us because we spared him."

Circling Hawk, who was Sitting Bull's good friend, spoke: "We trust Sitting Bull's wisdom in battle. We can trust his wisdom now. Let us do as he wishes."

Then Sitting Bull spoke again: "I have made him my brother. If you kill this boy, you kill my brother."

The little Assiniboine's life was spared, but No-Neck was not pleased. "Someday Sitting Bull will be sorry that he took an enemy into his tepee," No-Neck said angrily. "A rattlesnake would make a safer brother!"

No-Neck was wrong. When Sitting Bull married and had children, the Assiniboine boy loved them all. Life was happy inside the smoke-browned tepee. Each person tried to make the others feel as pleasant and warm as if the sunlight were upon them. In time the Assiniboine became one of the best hunters in the village. He was given the name of Kills-Often because he was a brave warrior.

The passing years brought more fame to Sitting Bull. He was the leader in his own village on the Grand River. In camps throughout the Sioux Nation, men talked of his deeds as they sat around dim fires in their tepees. They told how Sitting Bull was so strong he could shoot an arrow all the way through a buffalo and into the snow beyond. He was generous and shared his kills with others. And he honored the Animal People although he must kill them for food. When he saw buffalo bones lying on the prairie, he turned the skulls to face the warm sun, saying, "These are the bones of those who gave their flesh to keep us alive last winter."

They told how he captured many horses from enemy tribes and gave them away. He was a peace-maker in his camp. He was gentle to his family. No

A buffalo hunt. The shaggy beasts provided the
Plains Indians with food, shelter, clothing, and most
of the other necessities of daily life.

child feared him. He abolished slavery in his band and set many captives free. He told jokes and stories, and made up songs and drew pictures. He could think and speak wisely.

"*Hau*," they said around the tepee fires. "Yes. Most men act too quickly and are often sorry afterward. Sitting Bull is never heedless. He thinks ahead, and when he speaks, his words are wise."

5. The New Chief

Trouble came like a great black cloud over the tepees of the Sioux. Long ago the white men had moved onto the southern plains. Now they were beginning to come north into Sioux land!

"The white men's covered wagons roll across our country," No-Neck told the Hunkpapa warrior society. "Their soldiers build forts on Indian land. Their hunters kill so many buffalo that soon there will be none left to feed us."

"The white men make treaties and break them," said Circling Hawk. "Wherever the white men go, they take our hunting grounds, and the Indians lose their old free way of life. Our people are sent to live on reservations and be fed by Grandfather."

"Grandfather" was the Sioux name for the white men's government in Washington, D.C.

Not only the Hunkpapas were worried. All the branches of the Sioux nation were troubled. The black cloud hung above the camps of the Oglalas, Brulés, Miniconjous, and others.

Among themselves the people said, "Our nation is large, and our camps are far-scattered. We have many chiefs and many council fires. We need a leader who will join us all in one big council fire. We need a head chief—an *I-tan-chan*—for we must band together to save our land."

All the Sioux met together to choose an I-tan-chan. Five great camps were set up along the Grand River. Under shady trees hundreds of women and children passed pleasant days while the men sat in council.

Who should be I-tan-chan?

He must be a great-hearted man—generous, above spite and selfishness. He must forgive everything and never lose his temper. He must be a father to the whole tribe.

He must also be a man who honors Sioux law and customs, and who would keep safe the hunting grounds. He must be a man whom the white men could not cheat.

The Hunkpapa warrior society put up the name of Sitting Bull. Although he was very young to be I-tan-chan—only 35 winters old—he was quickly chosen.

Sitting Bull was named *I-tan-chan*, or head chief, of the entire Sioux Nation.

Then a group of sub-chiefs seated Sitting Bull on a buffalo robe. They gave him a bow and ten arrows, and a flintlock gun. A chief should be as powerful as an eagle, so they gave him a magnificent war-bonnet of black and white eagle feathers that reached from his head to the ground. They gave him a fine white horse. After all had smoked the long pipe around the council fire, they gave him the pipe as a badge of office. There were many brave speeches and songs. There was a parade with every warrior dressed in his best of fringe and bead and feather.

The sub-chief Four Horse was master of ceremonies. He made a speech in which he told Sitting Bull: "Because of your bravery on the battlefield, and your reputation as the bravest warrior in all our bands, we have chosen you head chief of the entire Sioux Nation. It is your duty to see that the nation is fed, that we have plenty. When you say 'fight' we shall fight, and when you say 'make peace' we shall make peace."

"Now tell us what we must do," the braves begged.

"You must be patient," answered Sitting Bull. "Someday we will have to fight a big war with the white men, but not yet. Let us keep peace as long as we can, so that our old men may sit in the sun and our children may play. Let us not make war until we must."

27

So it was settled on that fine bright day on the banks of the Grand River. The Sioux would keep peace with the white men as long as they could.

6. A Peace Treaty

Sitting Bull was camped near the Powder River in Montana when the Grandfather sent a man to see him. The man carried a message to Sitting Bull: "Come to Fort Laramie and sign a peace treaty. The Grandfather wants peace with you."

Sitting Bull sat looking out over the grassy plain. For a long time he did not answer the man. It was May, the month that the Indians called Moon of Thunderstorms. Sitting Bull's thoughts were like thunderstorms too.

"I have tried to keep peace, but the white men will not let me," he thought. "The whites have spread over Sioux hunting ground. They have plowed land and built fences. They have laid roads and cut timber and burned grass. They have killed much game and frightened more away."

The white men had many guns with which to fight. Yet in battle the Indians had taken many scalps. There had been much fighting lately. But fighting had not stopped the whites from coming into Sioux land. How could they be stopped?

At last Sitting Bull said to the messenger: "The Sioux also want peace, but not at the cost of their freedom. We will not go on a reservation and be treated like children.

"This land is ours. Much of it has already been taken from us, but we can feed ourselves if we are allowed to keep our Black Hills. Tell Grandfather that the Black Hills must be given to us in the treaty, or there will be no peace."

The messenger carried Sitting Bull's words to the Grandfather. The Grandfather knew without a peace treaty the Indians would attack more wagon trains and burn more military forts. They would kill and scalp. No white man would be safe on the northern plains. In time there would be all-out war.

The Grandfather decided it would be wise to give back to the Indians the hunting grounds that Sitting Bull wanted. The whites would still have much land that had once belonged to the Sioux. With the land divided between red men and white, both races could live peaceably.

Sitting Bull sent two of his chiefs to Fort Laramie. They were Gall and Bull Owl.

They signed the peace treaty. It was a good one. The Sioux were given a vast land of plains and forests in parts of what are now the states of Montana, Wyoming, Nebraska, and the Dakotas. The Black

At Fort Laramie (above) the Sioux signed a treaty which promised them the Black Hills forever.

Hills were also included. No white man could enter this land without the Indians' permission. The treaty was to last forever.

The treaty was a great victory for Sitting Bull, more than he had ever won in battle. He had won the victory by compromise, which meant giving up some of the hunting ground in order to keep the rest. And the Sioux had kept the best part—the Black Hills.

At last the Indians could be happy again, and live a life of freedom far away from the whites.

30

7. Broken Promises

One autumn day Chief Sitting Bull called twenty of his Hunkpapa warriors together. "Indians from Canada have been stealing our pony herds," he said. "We must teach them a lesson."

"*Hau*," agreed No-Neck. "We will get back our ponies."

The war party set out. It was autumn, the Moon of Yellow Leaves, and all the land was bright with color. Kills-Often rode beside Sitting Bull.

They found a small band of Canadian Indians driving the pony herd across the northern Montana plains. The Canadians fled, and Sitting Bull's men turned the ponies toward home.

Then without warning a large party of strange Indians attacked the Hunkpapas. The strangers had been hiding in a thick clump of trees. Their sudden charge took Sitting Bull's braves by surprise. Since they could not fight off so many men, the Hunkpapas knew they would all be killed.

Suddenly a new war party, whooping and waving lances, rode into the woods. It was a band of Assiniboines. Now the twenty Hunkpapas faced two bands of enemies!

"This battle will not last long," Sitting Bull told himself grimly.

But what was happening? The chief stared in astonishment. The Assiniboines were not fighting the Sioux! They were fighting side by side with the Sioux against the strangers!

When the strange warriors saw they were outnumbered, they gathered up their wounded and rapidly rode away. Sitting Bull and a few braves chased them until their painted ponies were lost among the trees.

When Sitting Bull rode back to the battle place, he found that the Assiniboines had also gone. He said, "I do not understand. Why should the Assiniboines help the Sioux?"

Kills-Often knew because he had talked to the Assiniboine leader. Now he explained to Sitting Bull: "My father's people say they are your friends. They say that long ago you showed mercy to an Assiniboine boy. Today when they saw the battle, they decided to thank you by fighting with you against the strangers."

A faraway look came into Sitting Bull's eyes. He remembered when Kills-Often stood in the snow with his small bow and arrow. He remembered the words: "Big brother."

No-Neck spoke. "We owe our lives to Sitting Bull's brother. We owe our lives to Kills-Often."

Several years passed. Chief Sitting Bull led his

warriors against other tribes, but never against the Assiniboines.

White men began to come into the treaty land without permission. Some were surveyors. They planned where to lay railroad tracks. Others were blue-coated soldiers of the United States cavalry. They rode into the Black Hills. They said they had discovered gold.

Gold! There was gold in the Black Hills! When white men heard that news, they rushed into the hills to find quick fortunes. They paid no attention to the peace treaty.

Sitting Bull's warriors tried to drive the gold miners away by attacking their camps and wagon trains. "The Black Hills belong to us!" the warriors cried.

To stop the trouble, Grandfather said he wanted to buy the Black Hills so that white people could live there.

Grandfather said the Indians could move to Standing Rock Agency in Dakota Territory. Then they would not need a hunting ground. On the reservation they would be fed by the government.

"We will not sell the Black Hills," Sitting Bull said angrily. "Let the white men keep the treaty they made with us."

The white men did not listen. They wanted gold.

8. The Camp on Rosebud River

Winter came. It was the Moon of Frost in the Tepee. Grandfather sent a message to Sitting Bull: "All the Sioux must go now to Standing Rock. You must live on the reservation. If you do not start at once, the blue-coated soldiers will come with their guns."

Nothing was said about the peace treaty. Grandfather had forgotten it.

The agency was 240 miles from Sitting Bull's Montana camp. The weather was bitterly cold. The chief could not take women and children on that hard journey.

The Grandfather was angry when the Sioux did not go to Standing Rock Agency. He ordered his soldiers to destroy their villages.

The soldiers rode out. Icy winds blew, and snow lay deep on the frozen ground. The soldiers returned to the agency. It was too cold for their horses to travel. Grandfather agreed that they could wait until warm spring days to attack the Indians.

Chief Sitting Bull had tried to keep the peace for eight years, but now he was angry. "The soldiers will come and attack us," he told his braves. "They want war. All right, we'll give it to them." When spring came he sent his runners to every Indian village with the words: "It is war. Come to my camp on the Rosebud River. Let us join together to fight the soldiers."

The Sioux went to Sitting Bull's camp. Among them were the Oglala Sioux, led by the brave war chief, Crazy Horse. All the free Indians left on the northern plains—Cheyenne, Arapaho, Blackfoot—also joined Sitting Bull. Their tepees stretched for miles along the river, for there were thousands of warriors and their families.

To the children it was like a holiday. They played in the warm sun under the blue sky. Sitting Bull's little daughters were there—Sleeping Water and Standing Holly. So was his small son, Crowfoot.

While the children played, their mothers cooked deer and buffalo meat. Sitting Bull's wife, Running Deer, picked wild strawberries. The warriors sat in council and smoked the war pipe. Sitting Bull was the leader.

"We must all stay together," he told them. "That is the way to win." He held up a finger. "One finger, see? It is nothing. But five fingers together—they make a fist!"

The warriors held a Sun Dance for four days to ask the Sun God to help them in the battle to come. Sitting Bull danced for two days and two nights. Then he had a vision, a dream. In the dream he saw white soldiers falling out of the sky into the Indians' camp. The soldiers had no ears.

"*Hau, hau, hau,*" the warriors said when he told them his dream. "The soldiers have no ears for they will not listen to the Indians. They do not hear what we say. That is why there is so much trouble."

A troop of United States cavalry under General George Crook rode up the valley of the Rosebud. The red men defeated it.

"Now we can go home," the braves said. "We have won."

"No," said Sitting Bull. "This is not the big battle

Sitting Bull danced the Sun Dance and had a vision of a great battle to come.

I saw in my dream. The soldiers have not fallen into our camp yet. If we go off in small bands, they will catch us and kill us easily. We must stay together. Remember the one finger!"

While they were waiting, the Indians moved their camp west to the valley of the Little Bighorn River. Their ponies had eaten all the grass along the Rosebud.

By now it was full summer, the Moon of Ripe Juneberries. In the beautiful Montana valley, they waited for the white soldiers to fall into their camp.

9. War on the Prairie

Fat Bear brought the news to Chief Sitting Bull. He said that scouts had seen a long line of soldiers riding into the valley. More soldiers were across the river.

The chief nodded. "They plan to come at us from two sides. They think they will catch us in a trap."

Quickly the word spread among the braves of the various tribes. They painted their faces with war paint and jumped on their ponies. Some went to fight the river soldiers. Others rode up the valley. They had no plan of attack. Each warrior rode where he wished.

A great stillness lay over the land on that afternoon of June 25, 1876. The 225 troopers of the Seventh

United States Cavalry moved quietly. They wanted to take the Indian village by surprise. Their banners drooped in the hot air. Dust rose behind the hoofs of their sweating horses.

Colonel George A. Custer was their leader. Sometimes he let his blond hair grow long enough to touch his shoulders, so the Indians called him "Long Hair." They hated him because he was the treaty-breaking officer who had led his soldiers into the Black Hills and had discovered gold.

The braves were as quiet as the troopers. When they saw the troopers, they hid from sight among the cottonwood trees. They had planned a surprise too.

Long Hair's men rode down a sunny slope and out upon the open plain. With a whoop the warriors left the trees and raced toward them. Crazy Horse, brave Oglala Sioux warrior, shouted: "It's a good day to fight! It's a good day to die!"

The noise of battle echoed across the land. Guns barked. Arrows whizzed. Horses snorted in fright, and men called out in anger or pain.

The white soldiers fought bravely, but there were too many Indians. It was the largest group of red warriors that had ever gathered on the Great Plains. Tomahawks flashed. Lances flew through the air. One by one Long Hair's troopers fell upon the prairie grass. In half an hour not a soldier was alive.

Colonel George A. Custer, well known to the Sioux
as an Indian fighter, led the cavalry at the Battle
of the Little Bighorn. This photograph of Custer
was taken during the Civil War, when he held the
temporary rank of a major general.

That night at the village the braves who had beaten Long Hair said proudly, "Now the white men will leave us alone!"

"*Hau*," agreed the braves who had whipped the river soldiers.

But Chief Sitting Bull's face was grave.

He knew that the victory had been too big. The Indians had killed too many whites. Grandfather would be so angry he would send an even larger army against them. No, thought Sitting Bull, now there could never be peace.

He called all the warriors together. He told them, "We must go far away from here. We have won a great victory, but it will do us no good. We must go to Canada, where we can find peace. There our women and children can lie down and feel safe."

The Hunkpapas agreed, but other Sioux said that Canada was too far away.

The next morning some of the braves wanted to find and fight some of the river soldiers who had escaped. "Let them live," said the chief. "They came against us, and we have killed all those who did not escape. That is enough."

Other braves went to the battlefield to take the belongings of Long Hair's slain troopers. Sitting Bull argued against this. He said that such looting would teach the Indians to want things that white men had.

The Indians could not agree where to live. So the bands scattered over the plains, and only Sitting Bull's Hunkpapas went with him to Canada. The Indians who stayed in the United States were soon forced to go on reservations, and the Black Hills became the property of white men.

10. A Rough Trail

Chief Sitting Bull and his followers lived peacefully in Canada for over five years. Representatives of the United States and Canadian governments tried to get them to return to their own country.

Sitting Bull would not agree to return and surrender. He would only talk. He knew that the longer he talked, the longer his people could stay safely in Canada. He would gladly have talked forever.

Yet in time the Hunkpapas grew homesick. They missed the rolling plains they had loved. They wanted to see the Black Hills again. Often they were hungry because there were no buffalo to hunt. At last Sitting Bull led them home.

On a hot summer morning in 1881, he surrendered to army officers at Fort Buford in the Dakotas.

He was 50 years old now, and his black hair was streaked with gray. His shirt and leggings were dusty from the long trip across the plains. He was tired,

Sitting Bull and Buffalo Bill, photographed at a performance of the Wild West Show

and his heart was sad, yet he had all the dignity of a great Sioux chief.

He gave his rifle to his little boy, Crowfoot, to hand to the white men. Then Sitting Bull proudly said: "Let it be recorded that I was the last man of my people to lay down my gun."

The Hunkpapas were put on the Standing Rock reservation. They lived in huts, and they planted patches of corn. They were given some food and clothing, but not enough. Many times they were cold and hungry.

Sitting Bull was saddened by the suffering of his people. He did all he could to get better treatment for them.

One summer he was invited to be part of Buffalo Bill's Wild West Show. Cowboys and Indians were in the show, and there was much fast riding and noisy gunfire. Sitting Bull rode a big gray horse. Around and around the arena he rode, wearing his beaded deerskin clothes and a great feather war-bonnet.

The white people stared hard at him. They remembered that he had led the Indians in the big battle when Colonel Custer's 225 troopers were slain. Many people hissed at him. Many shouted, "Custer's killer!"

Sitting Bull did not enjoy performing, but he did so because he was paid well. His people needed the money he could send to them. The few pennies he had left over he gave to small ragged boys that he saw in the cities. They were white boys but they needed help, and he helped them.

Buffalo Bill's show was asked to visit England. Sitting Bull said he would not go. "It is bad for the Indians' cause for me to parade around," he said. "I have learned that it awakens the hatred of white people. Besides, I am needed on the reservation."

Buffalo Bill gave Sitting Bull the big gray horse

A dejected Sitting Bull was photographed at Standing Rock Reservation in 1882 with his wife and three of his children. The names of the other woman and child are not known.

that he had ridden. Sitting Bull took it home with him. He and the circus horse were friends, just as he had been friends with the Animal People and the Bird People in the old free days on the plains.

11. Battle in the Dark

Slowly the years passed. They were bitter ones for the Sioux. Often the people were near starvation.

Sitting Bull lived in a log cabin on the Grand River, near where he was born. He raised a few chickens and tended a corn patch. His chief interest was in helping his people.

He wanted the government to build schools for the children and to teach the men to farm. Little was done.

Then hope came to the despairing Indians in a new religion. It was called the Ghost Dance. Far west in Nevada a Paiute Indian named Wovoka said the people must sing special sacred songs and do a special dance. Then the dead warriors would rise, the white men would leave the country. The buffalo would come back.

It was like a wonderful dream to the Indians. They sang songs and danced the Ghost Dance.

"Soon now, soon," they whispered to each other. They watched for their dead to come back to life.

They sent young men out to scout for the first sign of returning buffalo.

Word of the new religion reached Standing Rock. Many Sioux believed Wovoka. Sitting Bull did not. "It is impossible for a dead man to return and live again," he said.

The government worried that there might be an Indian uprising. Agents went to see Sitting Bull about the Ghost Dances.

"Why don't you go to Nevada and talk to Wovoka?" Sitting Bull asked. "Find out about this religion so that my people can be told the truth." The white men said they were too busy to go.

Still the government worried. Agents thought that Sitting Bull himself might lead an uprising. In the winter of 1890, the government ordered his arrest.

By performing the Ghost Dance, Indians hoped to return to their days of glory.

Forty Indian policemen went to the log cabin early one morning before dawn. They were young men who cooperated with the whites in order to be given special privileges. They felt important at arresting so great a chief. Lieutenant Bullhead was their leader. They entered the cabin and pulled Sitting Bull roughly from his bed.

"We have come for you. If you fight you will be killed," they said.

"*Hau, hau.* You come for me, I am going," answered the chief.

His old wife went out into the dark. "Saddle the gray horse," she told her sons. Many sleeping nearby heard the noise. They gathered in front of the cabin. Kills-Often was there. He forced his way in to protect his brother.

A murmur of anger went through the crowd when they saw the policemen shove the old chief through the door. Sitting Bull grew angry too. He had said he would go, but he did not intend to be pushed and shoved.

Suddenly he rebelled. He shouted to the policemen, "I am not going. Do with me what you like. I am not going."

One of Sitting Bull's friends fired a shot. It hit Lieutenant Bullhead. As he fell dying, he shot Sitting Bull.

Then there was shooting everywhere. The night blazed with gunfire. The old gray circus horse, standing saddled by the door, pricked up his ears. He thought he was back in the Wild West Show.

The horse began to do his tricks. He bowed. He sat back on his haunches and lifted one foot as he had been taught to do in the circus.

For a moment the policemen were frightened. They thought the spirit of the dead Sitting Bull had gone into the sitting horse.

The battle was soon over. Fourteen men lay dead or dying on the frozen ground. Some were policemen, some were Sitting Bull's people. His son Crowfoot had been killed. So had his loyal brother Kills-Often. Somebody led the old gray horse back to the barn.

Sitting Bull was 59 years old when he died. For almost 25 years he had been the greatest leader of the greatest Indian nation. He was a fierce warrior and a gentle friend. He was a statesman and a prophet.

He was the strongest and boldest of his race, and today he is the best-remembered Indian who ever lived.

In the Words of Sitting Bull

"When I was a boy, the Sioux owned the world; the sun rose and set on their land; they sent ten thousand men to battle. Where are the warriors today? Who slew them? Where are our lands? Who owns them? . . . Is it wrong for me to love my own? Is it wicked for me because my skin is red? Because I am a Sioux; because I was born where my father lived; because I would die for my people and my country?"

"If the Great Spirit had desired me to be a white man he would have made me so in the first place. He put in your heart certain wishes and plans, in my heart he put other and different desires. Each man is good in his sight. It is not necessary for eagles to be crows."

50

About Sitting Bull's People

The Hunkpapa Sioux lived in the hills and on the plains of the area known today as Nebraska and South Dakota. They were known as brave warriors, hunters of buffalo, and expert horsemen. The Sioux did not establish permanent villages. In the winter they lived in small bands in river valleys; in the summer these bands joined together and moved onto the plains in search of buffalo. When a herd was located, they set up their tepee villages, and the hunt was on! Buffalo provided the Hunkpapas—and all Sioux—with food, clothing, shelter, tools, and weapons. The map below shows where Sitting Bull grew to manhood and fought the battles which determined his nation's fate.

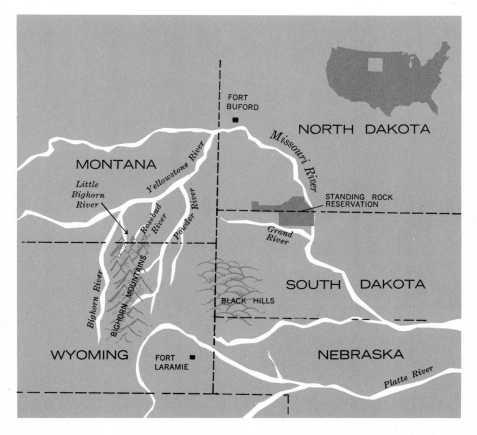

There is no known picture of Crazy Horse. The Indian
warrior shown above is a detail from the painting
entitled *Custer's Last Stand* by William Leigh.

Crazy Horse

Warrior Chief of the Sioux

by Enid LaMonte Meadowcroft

"This is a good day to die!" cried Crazy Horse. "Follow me!" With these words, the great Sioux warrior chief led his people into their very last battle. His desperate fight against the miners and settlers who were destroying the Indian way of life was almost at an end.

53

1. An Invitation

Curly pulled back hard on his bowstring. He let his arrow fly. It hit a tree and stuck fast. Curly spoke to the tall Indian standing beside him.

"Was that good, Hump?" he asked. "Will I be ready soon to hunt buffalo?"

Hump smiled. "No boy can hunt buffalo," he said. "You must wait until you can use a stronger bow. Come, we'll go back to the village now."

Curly pulled his arrow from the tree and followed Hump. He tried to walk through the woods silently, as Hump did.

"When I grow up," he thought, "I want to be called Crazy Horse like my father. But I want to be a warrior like Hump."

Soon he and Hump reached the village. The Oglala Indians were living in a big circle of tepees on the Niobrara River. The Niobrara is in Nebraska. In 1851, when Curly was nine, Nebraska was Indian country. Buffalo roamed over the plains. Wild horses grazed on the hills.

The Oglalas depended on the buffalo for food

and hides. They followed the great herds from place to place. When they moved their village they needed many horses, so they caught the wild horses and tamed them. Sometimes they took horses from other tribes.

Curly had his own pony. One day he went off to hunt rabbits. When he came back his sister, Bright Star, ran to meet him.

"There's a meeting at the council tepee," she cried. "Chief Smoke wants to talk to us about the white men. Hurry!"

"White men!" Curly jumped from his pony.

He had seen white men at their fort. It was near their road which crossed the Indians' hunting grounds. Curly liked the whites and wanted to hear about them. He ran to the big tepee.

A large crowd had gathered around it. Curly sat down with his mother and his brother, Little Hawk. The sides of the big tepee were rolled up. Inside he could see his father talking with Chief Smoke. Crazy Horse was the Oglalas' holy man and gave them good advice. At last Smoke stood up.

"A message has come from the white men," he said. "We have all been invited to their fort. Other tribes will be there. The white men want to talk to our chiefs. They will give us all presents. Shall we go?"

"Yes!" cried many of the people gathered outside.
"No!" cried several of the warriors.

One of them jumped to his feet. "We should have nothing to do with those whites," he shouted. "They give us their white-man sickness. They frighten away our buffalo. We must drive them out before it is too late."

He sat down, and everyone began to talk at once. Curly's heart was beating like a drum. Chief Smoke spoke again.

"We have plenty of buffalo," Smoke said quietly. "And there are not many whites. I think we should

Curly's people moved their belongings quickly from place to place on travois pulled by dogs and horses.

go to their fort. We should find out why they want to talk to us and give us presents."

"Yes," cried the people. "We will go."

The next morning they took down their tepees and loaded them on their travois. A travois was made of two long poles, with nets of rawhide slung between them. One end of the travois was harnessed to a packhorse or a dog. The other end dragged on the ground.

When all the travois were loaded, the Oglalas set out. Five days later they reached Fort Laramie on the Platte River.

Other bands of Indians had already arrived. They all belonged to the Sioux, or Dakota, Nation. Their tepees and horse herds were spread out far over the plains around Fort Laramie.

Curly was surprised by the number. "I didn't know there were so many of us in all the world," he thought proudly. "Why should any Indians want to drive away a few white men?"

2. Curly Hunts Buffalo

Curly had a good time at Fort Laramie. He and his friends watched the soldiers drill. They raced their ponies along the white-man road. They played war games with boys of other tribes.

One day 27 big wagons rolled into the Indians' great encampment.

"They are bringing the presents from the White Father in Washington," Curly told his friend, Lone Bear. "My father says they were sent because our chiefs signed a promise paper."

"What did they promise?" asked Lone Bear.

"To let the white men build more forts along their road," Curly answered. "And not to hurt white travelers. Then the whites promised to give us presents every year for 50 years."

The Indians crowded around the wagons. Soon the presents were handed out. There were hatchets, knives, bolts of red cloth, beads, and other things.

Curly's present was a small mirror. It was like the signal mirrors which the warriors used.

Before long the Oglalas returned to their own buffalo country. Then Curly practiced flashing mirror signals in the sun. His father made him a strong, new bow. He practiced with that too.

One evening his father called him into their tepee. Hump was there.

"We've been talking about you, Curly," said his father. "You are ten winters old. It's time you decided what you want to be when you're a man."

"A warrior," Curly replied promptly. "The bravest in the tribe."

Like most Sioux boys, Curly learned at an early age
how to capture wild horses and tame them.

Both men smiled. Curly was small for his age.
His hair and skin were lighter than those of most
Indians. This made him look weak. But Crazy Horse
and Hump knew that he was strong and wiry.

"Very well," said his father. "Hump has offered to
train you. But you must work hard."

"I will work hard," Curly promised, and he did.

Hump taught him to shoot at a target while riding
on his pony. He trained Curly to run long distances
without stopping to rest. Sometimes Hump made

Curly fast for a day and go without water. He gave the boy a wild horse and told him how to tame her.

When Curly was eleven, Hump took him on a buffalo hunt. Hump led the other hunters. Curly rode beside him. At the top of a hill, they stopped. The plain below them was dark with buffalo. Hump gave a signal.

"*Hoka hey!*" cried the hunters. "Let's go."

They galloped toward the buffalo. Curly aimed at a calf, but his arrow hit a large bull. The animal charged at him. Curly wanted to gallop away, but he sent two more arrows into the bull.

The angry animal still came toward him, faster and faster. Curly shot again. The bull sank to the ground and died.

The other hunters killed many buffalo. That night there was a feast in the village. Then some of the warriors walked around the big circle of tepees. Each one sang of a brave deed he had done that day. Hump sang about Curly.

"On his first hunt," sang Hump, "he bravely killed an angry bull. Let us call out his name."

"Curly! Curly!" called the people. "Stand out where we can see you."

But Curly sat hidden in the shadow of his father's tepee. "It is not much to kill a buffalo," he thought. "Someday I must do things which are braver still."

3. A Runaway Cow

The Oglalas went twice to Fort Laramie to get their presents. The third time they went the presents did not come. They waited many days. So did other Sioux Indians.

Curly did not like waiting. He wanted to get back to the buffalo country. One hot day he stood by the white-man road, watching a wagon train roll by. Walking behind the wagons was a white man driving an old cow.

Suddenly five boys from the Brulé tribe came racing toward the road. Each tried to reach it first. They yelled and whipped up their ponies.

The noise frightened the cow. She bolted into the Brulé village. Darting into a tepee, she came out with a bundle stuck on her horns.

Curly and the Brulé boys, shouting with glee, chased her. On the cow ran, knocking over a kettle of stew, and kicking up a big cloud of dust.

Dogs barked. Men laughed. Women and children scrambled out of her way.

"Shoot her," cried an old woman. "She'll hurt someone."

A warrior named Straight Foretop quickly shot the cow. The owner of the cow hurried to Fort Laramie. He reported that the Indians had stolen his cow and killed her.

Soon bad news reached the Indians. Soldiers were coming from the fort to arrest Straight Foretop and put him in jail.

"For shooting a *cow!*" Curly could not believe it. To take away an Indian's freedom was a terrible punishment. Nothing could be worse.

"No whites will ever lock *me* up in a box with iron bars," Curly said to Lone Bear. "I'd kill anyone who tried."

The boys waited outside the Brulé village and watched for the soldiers. They came at last, led by an officer named Grattan.

Grattan did not like Indians. He could not speak their language. So he had brought an interpreter named Wyuse. Wyuse was drunk.

The village seemed empty. Not an Indian was in sight. Wyuse galloped around the circle of tepees.

"Come out, you red devils," he yelled. "We'll kill you like dogs."

Chief Conquering Bear stepped from his tepee. He walked bravely toward Grattan.

"Don't hurt my people," he said quietly. "We can settle this matter peacefully, my friend. We will give you five fine horses to pay for that cow."

The chief waited for Wyuse to put his words into white-man language. No one knows what Wyuse said. Suddenly Grattan shouted an order. His soldiers raised their guns and shot Conquering Bear. Instantly the village was filled with angry warriors. Grattan and his men tried to flee, but the warriors chased them and killed every one.

Curly had never seen men killed before. It made him feel sick and not at all brave.

The Indians did not want more trouble with the white men. They packed up their tepees. By nightfall they were heading for the hills.

4. "I Hate the Whites"

Curly's mother was a Brulé Indian. She missed her own people. So Curly's family traveled with the Brulés for a while. The Brulés set up their tepees on Blue Water Creek. It was a long way from Fort Laramie.

Curly missed Hump, but he was happy. A year passed. Then a terrible thing happened.

Soldiers from the fort came to punish the Brulés for killing Grattan and his men. They surprised the peaceful village. The warriors had no time to arm themselves. Many men, women, and children were killed. Others were carried off to the jail at Fort Laramie.

Curly was away that day, hunting in the sand hills. In the evening he rode home. There he saw the bodies on the ground. Curly looked swiftly for his father and mother, for Little Hawk and Bright Star. They were not there.

Then he saw moccasin tracks leading north, and he knew that some Indians had escaped. He followed the tracks.

Suddenly he heard a woman crying. He found her hiding in some bushes, holding a tiny baby in her arms.

"They have killed my husband," she sobbed, "and my little boy. I am too sick to walk, too sick to ride. I will die here with my baby."

"No," said Curly. "I'll help you."

He had seen a broken travois on the trail. He ran back to get it and hitched it to his horse. Carefully he put the woman onto it. Then he went on, leading his horse.

The moon shone dimly. All night he followed the tracks of the fleeing Indians. At dawn he found the people, camping beside a lake. His family was there, caring for the wounded. Little Hawk told him about the attack.

Curly grew hot with anger as he listened. He remembered the women and children he had seen, lying dead on the ground. He thought of the people who had been carried off to jail. He remembered the shooting of brave Conquering Bear.

"Why do they do these terrible things to us?" he cried. "I hate the whites! I hate them!"

He hoped that some warriors would rescue the people in the fort jail. But the Brulés were not strong enough now to send out a war party against the whites. When the wounded could travel, they all moved farther north.

Curly and his family stayed with them for nearly two years. Then they went to live again with the Oglalas.

5. Curly Wins His Name

The Oglalas were living near the Powder River in Montana. Curly was glad to be with them again.

One morning he saw Hump and other warriors putting on war paint and feathers.

"Where are you going?" he asked Hump. "Against an enemy tribe?"

"Yes," said Hump. "It's a strange tribe. They are grass-house people. They have many horses. We're going to take some."

"Please take me with you," Curly said quickly.

Hump looked him over. Curly was seventeen now. He was still small for his age. But he had worked hard to learn all that a good warrior should know.

"All right," said Hump. "Get your weapons."

Curly ran for his bow and arrows and his horse. His heart pounded with excitement. This was his first war party.

The grass-house warriors knew the Oglalas were coming. Their scouts had told them. They were waiting on a high hill, behind large rocks. Many of them had guns.

Some of the Oglalas had guns too. They circled the hill, whooping and shooting. Then they tried to ride to the top. But the enemy drove them back. Finally the Oglalas gathered some distance away to plan their next move.

Suddenly Curly left them. He galloped toward the hill and straight up the side. Bullets and arrows flew all around him. Still he rode on.

A grass-house warrior rose from a gully and aimed a gun at his head. Curly shot him quickly. Whirling around, he killed another warrior who was sneaking up behind him.

The Oglalas below sent up a great cheer. Curly slid from his horse and scalped the dead men. More bullets flew around him. An arrow hit him in the leg. He looked for his horse. The animal had bolted. Limping badly, Curly scrambled down the hill.

Hump met him with another horse. They rode away from the fighting. Hump cut the arrow from Curly's leg.

"You did well," he said. "While you kept the enemy busy, our men took some fine horses. Now you are a warrior. I'm proud of you."

Curly smiled. Although his leg hurt badly, he was happy.

That night the Oglalas had a big celebration. The warriors danced around the village campfire. Each one told of a brave deed he had done that day. Then it was Curly's turn to tell about his part in the battle. But he could not talk about himself before so many people.

So his father, wrapped in his holy blanket, stepped into the firelight. He walked slowly around the circle, singing:

Today, my son has fought bravely
against a strange tribe.
He has become a man and earned a
man's name.
I give him the great name my father
gave to me.
I give him the name Crazy Horse.

The people fell into line behind him. As they circled the campfire, they chanted the name of their brave new warrior.

"Crazy Horse! Crazy Horse! Crazy Horse!"

6. A Brave Decoy

Six years passed. The Oglalas stayed in the Powder River country. They had more fights with enemy tribes. Young Crazy Horse became one of their bravest warriors.

Meanwhile, Indians to the south were having trouble with the white men. Many settlers and soldiers had moved into their country near the Platte River. Most of the whites treated the Indians badly. They were afraid of them.

Sometimes they killed Indians who were their friends. Early one morning 700 soldiers attacked a village of peaceful Cheyenne Indians. It was a surprise attack. Most of the Cheyennes were killed. Only a few escaped.

Runners quickly carried the news to the Powder River country. In every Sioux village, angry warriors gathered up their weapons. Then they rode south to punish the whites.

On a hot July morning a large war party rode quietly toward a fort on the Platte River. Hump was leading it. Crazy Horse was one of the party.

Two miles from the fort, the warriors reached some sand hills.

"Hide in these hills," Hump told them. "Our brave decoys will go to the fort. They'll trick the soldiers

This cavalry attack on a peaceful Cheyenne village
would be remembered as the Sand Creek Massacre.

into coming out and lead them back here. When
the soldiers are close enough, I'll give a signal. Then
you must all rush out together and surround them."

The warriors hid. Crazy Horse and three other
decoys rode on. Some mules were grazing near the
fort. The decoys pretended that they were going to
steal them. A sentry shouted. The fort gates swung
open. Out rode 60 soldiers.

They fired at the decoys and chased them part
way to the sand hills. Crazy Horse saw them start
to turn back.

Quickly he slid from his horse. Crouching down,

he examined her foot. He pretended it was hurt. With a shout the soldiers rode toward him. He leaped into his saddle and galloped ahead.

Bullets whistled past his ears. The soldiers were close behind him. He led them nearer to the sand hills. They were almost near enough to be trapped.

But suddenly some of the warriors broke out of hiding. With shrill war cries they rushed at the enemy. The soldiers turned swiftly and galloped back to the fort.

Crazy Horse was hot with anger.

"You are like children," he shouted at the warriors. "Each of you wants to prove how brave he is. So you won't wait for your signal. The white men wait. They obey orders. They fight together. That's why they're strong."

Some of the warriors laughed at this. But the rest were ashamed. The next day the brave decoys lured the soldiers from the fort with another trick. This time the warriors waited. They rushed out from their hiding places together, and killed most of the soldiers.

"It is good to listen to Crazy Horse," the warriors agreed. "He is wise."

The Oglala chiefs were pleased with Crazy Horse, too. They gave him a beautiful beaded shirt and a fine new horse. They told him that he was now a leader of the tribe.

7. Crazy Horse Is Doubtful

White men soon pushed right into the Powder River country. They wanted to dig for gold in the Big Horn Mountains.

Miners' wagons, rattling along the trail to the mountains, scared the buffalo. Soldiers built a fort near the river. It was called Fort Phil Kearny.

In December of 1866, many Sioux warriors banded together to attack the fort. Crazy Horse led the decoys. Before the attack he spoke to the warriors. He reminded them of what had happened at the fort near the Platte.

"This is a larger fort," he said. "There are many more soldiers to be trapped. I'll wave a blanket over my head when it's time for you to break out of hiding. Wait for that signal, or all will be spoiled."

"We'll wait," the warriors promised. And they did.

The battle was a fierce one. Though the soldiers fought bravely, many were killed. But this did not discourage the white men.

"They are running over our land like ants," Crazy Horse said to his father one day in spring. "If we don't stop the whites now, more will come, and more and more."

He painted a yellow streak on his cheek and stuck a feather in his hair. Then he picked up his weapons and strode from the tepee. Soon he was leading a large war party toward the Bozeman Trail.

Sitting Bull and Red Cloud, leaders of other Sioux tribes, also led warriors against the whites. The Indians attacked wagon trains and stagecoaches. They burned miners' shacks. They stole horses and cattle. They killed travelers. No white man felt safe.

One warm summer day an Indian who was friendly to the whites rode into the Oglalas' village. He brought them a message from the soldiers at Fort Laramie.

The Sioux tried to stop the flow of whites to their lands by attacking stagecoaches and wagon trains.

"The whites are tired of fighting," he told the Oglalas. "If you will stop it, they will give you fine presents."

"We don't want presents," cried Crazy Horse angrily. "We want the whites to get out of our country. Tell them we'll fight until they do."

Other Sioux leaders sent the same message. So the whites decided to give up. In August 1867, the soldiers left Fort Phil Kearny. Sitting quietly on their horses, hundreds of warriors watched them ride away. Then joyfully, the warriors set fire to the fort and burned it to the ground.

The Sioux had won a big victory. The Oglalas sent Chief Red Cloud to Fort Laramie to put his mark on a peace treaty with the whites. He was proud and happy when he returned.

"The whites have promised to stay out of the Powder River country forever," he announced. "And they have promised that as long as grass grows and water flows, the country shall be ours."

Crazy Horse smiled doubtfully. He wondered how long the whites would keep their promise.

8. "Be Strong. Follow Me"

Crazy Horse was glad that he could stop fighting whites. Now he was free to do other things. Before long he married a fine young woman named Black Shawl. A baby daughter was born to them, and for nearly four years they were happy.

Then their little girl died of the white man's coughing disease. Soon after that, the whites broke their promise.

Again miners and soldiers streamed into the Powder River country. This time they were after gold in the Black Hills. Crazy Horse led many war parties out to drive them away, but the whites came on like a flood.

Soon an Indian messenger from Fort Laramie rode into the Oglala village.

"The White Father in Washington wants to buy the Black Hills," he told the Oglalas.

"We won't sell them," replied Crazy Horse quietly. "The Great Spirit gave them to us to keep."

Another messenger went to talk to Sitting Bull. He also refused to sell the hills. But Chief Red Cloud agreed to sell if he could get a good price. So did another chief named Spotted Tail.

Crazy Horse could not understand these two leaders. They had grown friendly with the whites. Now they were living with their people on reservations near Fort Laramie.

On the reservations they had to obey white soldiers. They had to eat food given to them by whites.

Colonel Custer led this expedition of miners and soldiers into the sacred Black Hills of the Sioux.

They could not hunt buffalo without permission. They could no longer roam where they pleased.

"A reservation is like a jail without walls," Crazy Horse said to Black Shawl. "I'll never live in a jail. I'd rather die."

Black Shawl nodded and choked back a cough. She, too, had caught the white man's terrible coughing sickness. When winter came her cough grew worse.

Crazy Horse hated to leave her. But he had to lead war parties against the miners. One snowy night he returned late to the village. A friend rode to meet him.

"A man from Fort Laramie came today," he said. "The whites are angry because we won't sell the hills. Now they say that all Indians must move out of the Powder River country. We must go to the reservations near the fort. If we don't go soon, they will send a big army against us. What shall we do?"

"We'll fight for our country," said Crazy Horse.

He knew that Sitting Bull would decide to fight too.

"Our people will be stronger if we're together," he thought.

So he led the Oglalas north to Sitting Bull's camp. It was in the valley near the Rosebud River.

Through the winter and spring, other Indians joined them there.

The camp in the valley of the Rosebud grew larger every day. The people enjoyed being together. They seemed to forget about the white men. But Crazy Horse and Sitting Bull did not forget. Their scouts were out, day and night, watching for the enemy.

One June evening Crazy Horse heard a sound in the distance like a wolf howling. It was a scout signaling danger. Crazy Horse called all the people to the council lodge. The scout arrived and spoke to them.

"The Rosebud is black with soldiers," he said.

"Three Stars leads them. They are only one sleep away."

"*Hopo!*" cried a warrior. "Let's go and fight them."

"No!" shouted another. "Wait here for them. We must stay to protect the helpless ones."

Now everyone began to talk at once. The old chiefs did not know what to do. Then Crazy Horse stood up.

"Some warriors will stay here to protect our women and children," he said. "I will lead the others against the white men. Their army is large and very strong. But if we fight together, we can win. All who are coming with me, get ready."

Nearly a thousand warriors hurried to get weapons and horses. An hour later they set out with Crazy Horse.

They traveled all night. Early in the morning they reached a ridge of hills near the Rosebud River. The warriors rode quietly to the top. There below them was the camp of General Crook, whom the Indians called Three Stars.

His soldiers did not know the Indians were near. Then one of Crook's scouts shouted an alarm. The soldiers ran for their guns and horses. Down the ridge rode the warriors, and the fight began.

The Sioux fought fiercely. So did the whites. Once some of the warriors fell back before the whites'

General George Crook. His troops had the assignment of moving Plains Indians onto reservations.

far-shooting guns. Crazy Horse rode quickly to stop them.

"Stand fast!" he cried. "Remember the helpless ones at home! Be strong! Follow me!"

Boldly he rode toward the enemy. The warriors followed him, and the fighting began again. The battle lasted almost all day. Finally the whites gave up. They retreated toward the south.

Crazy Horse and his warriors did not go after them. They had no bullets left and only a few arrows. Eight Indians had been killed, and some others were wounded. The warriors put the dead and the wounded in travois. Then they started slowly back to the encampment.

They had won a great victory. But Crazy Horse could not rejoice. He felt sure there would soon be more fighting. Two days later, he and Sitting Bull led all their people farther west.

9. Terrible Times

The Indians set up their tepees along the Little Bighorn River in Montana. There was good grass for the horses. The hunters brought in plenty of meat. Five days passed peacefully.

On the next day—June 25, 1876—the morning was hot. Children splashed in the river. Women worked at their easiest tasks. Men loafed in the shade.

Suddenly a scout galloped into the encampment.

"Soldiers are coming!" he cried. "Many soldiers!"

At once the camp was filled with confusion. Women called their children. They grabbed their babies and fled to the hills. Boys raced to drive in the horses. Warriors ran for their weapons. Each man seized the first horse that came along and rode out to meet the soldiers.

Crazy Horse called them to him.

"Be strong!" he shouted. "Fight together! *Hoka hey!*"

The soldiers were shooting into the camp. Suddenly Crazy Horse gave a signal. With wild cries the warriors charged. Slowly the soldiers fell back. Most

This version of the Battle of the Little Bighorn was painted about twenty years after the battle by Kicking Bear, who had fought there as a Sioux warrior. Custer (1) is pictured in buckskins and with the long hair which gave him his nickname.

The group of four figures (2) represents the victorious Sioux (left to right): Sitting Bull, Rain-in-the-Face (a Sioux chief), Crazy Horse, and the artist, Kicking Bear. In the lower right-hand corner, Sioux women are awaiting the return of the warriors in their village on the Bighorn.

of them were shot down. The rest fled. Then there was another alarm.

"More soldiers! Down the river! On the other side!"

"It's a good day to fight! It's a good day to die!" cried Crazy Horse.

Waving his rifle over his head, he galloped down the riverbank. Whooping warriors raced after him. Sitting Bull was leading warriors too. Whipping up their horses, they all crossed the river.

On came the soldiers. They were led by Colonel Custer, whom the Indians called Long Hair. After a hard fight, the Indians surrounded them. Custer and his men fought bravely. But when the battle ended every one of them was dead.

Many Indians had been killed or wounded. There was weeping in the camp that night. The next day scouts signaled that more soldiers were coming with cannon.

Crazy Horse knew that the warriors could not fight again so soon. Quickly the Indians loaded their travois and started north. Before long Crazy Horse and Sitting Bull decided to separate.

"That will make it harder for the soldiers to find us," they told their people.

So the great Sioux encampment was broken up. Each tribe went its own way. But wherever the Indians went, the soldiers tracked them down. There was more fighting. The noise of battle drove many buffalo away.

Winter came. It was bitter cold. The Indians did not have enough meat. They needed hides for new tepees and robes.

Now and then messengers from Fort Laramie rode into the Oglalas' village.

"Come to Red Cloud Reservation," they said. "The white men will give you blankets and plenty of food. They will give you new tents. Surrender and come to Red Cloud."

"And lose our freedom?" Crazy Horse answered angrily. "No!"

Weeks passed, and things grew worse. Sitting Bull's people fled to Canada to escape from the soldiers. But the Oglalas could not travel so far. They had no ammunition, and many were sick.

Often Crazy Horse left the village. Alone on the top of a little hill, he talked to the Great Spirit.

"Help me plan for my people," he begged. "Show me how to save them."

One spring evening he walked into his tepee and spoke to Black Shawl.

"I have hated the whites ever since they shot Conquering Bear," he said quietly. "I'd rather die than surrender to them. But, to save my people, I must lead them to Red Cloud."

10. A Sad Ending

In May the Oglalas went to Red Cloud. A large crowd of whites waited at Fort Robinson near the reservation to watch them arrive.

Crazy Horse led the long procession. As he rode past the whites on his big warhorse, he looked straight ahead.

At the reservation all the Indians dismounted. Soldiers took away their horses and weapons. The women put up the tepees. And the wild, free life of the Oglalas was ended.

Crazy Horse made sure they were all given food. Then he went to his own tepee. He was worried about Black Shawl. Her cough was so bad he was afraid she might die. Her people lived on the Spotted Tail Reservation, and she wanted to see them. So they set out together early in September.

Crazy Horse did not have permission to leave. The officers at Fort Robinson were afraid he'd stir up the Spotted Tail Indians. "He'll get them to join our Oglalas," one said, "and lead them against us. We must stop him."

Scouts were sent at once to catch Crazy Horse and arrest him. But he and his wife reached Spotted Tail safely. An officer named Lee met them. Crazy Horse explained why they had come.

"Your wife may stay," said Major Lee. "But you must go back tomorrow. You may tell the general at Fort Robinson what you've told me. No harm will come to you."

"That is good," said Crazy Horse wearily. "I don't want to make trouble. I only want peace."

The next day he was taken to Fort Robinson. The general would not see him. Another officer shook his hand.

"Come with me," he said. "I'll show you where to spend the night."

Crazy Horse walked quietly with him past some armed guards and through a door. Suddenly he jumped back. Ahead of him was what he hated most—a white-man jail! Whirling around, he pulled out his knife. Guards grabbed his arms.

"Let me go!" he cried, fighting with all his might to get away. "Let me go!"

"Kill him!" shouted the officer.

A soldier with a bayonet lunged toward Crazy Horse and stabbed him in the back. The great warrior staggered and sank to the ground. Before morning he was dead.

He had fought bravely to hold his country and to keep his people free. He lost the fight. But today Americans speak of him proudly and remember the name of a great leader—Crazy Horse.

In the Words of Crazy Horse

"The Great Spirit gave us this country as a home. You had yours. We did not interfere with you. The Great Spirit gave us plenty of land to live on, and buffalo, deer, antelope, and other game. But you have come here; you are taking my land from me; you are killing off our game, so it is hard for us to live. Now, you tell us to work for a living, but the Great Spirit did not make us to work, but to live by hunting. . . . Again you say, why do you not become civilized? We do not want your civilization! We would live as our fathers did, and their fathers before them."

"One does not sell the earth on which the people walk."

About Crazy Horse's People

The Oglalas were, like the Hunkpapas, a branch of the Sioux or Dakota Nation. They too lived in what is today South Dakota and Nebraska. They were a nomadic people who hunted buffalo on horseback and fought their enemies bravely. Their way of life, like that of the other Plains Indians, was completely dependent on the buffalo. The map below includes the Black Hills, where Crazy Horse's people lived, and the Bighorn River area, where they fought their last great battle.

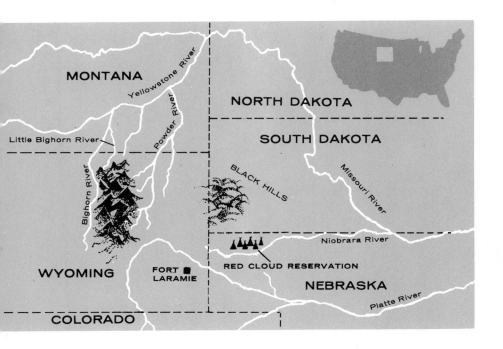

Quanah Parker

Last Comanche War Chief

by LaVere Anderson

Defiant Quanah, half-white and half-Comanche, vowed never to take his band of Comanches onto a reservation. Quanah's braves took to the war road to stop white buffalo hunters from destroying the herds on the Staked Plains. But time was running out for the buffalo and for Quanah. He was the last chief of his tribe to surrender.

89

1. White Man's Blood

Quanah watched the other boys swimming and splashing in the Llano River. The Indians called it the River of Wild Hogs because long ago a brave had killed a wild hog on the bank. Quanah did not join in the boys' fun.

Instead, he sat in the water scrubbing himself with a handful of rough weeds. He had already scrubbed so hard that his skin felt sore.

"Look at Quanah!" Little Cloud shouted. "He is trying to wash away his white man's smell."

"Quanah! Quanah!" the others cried. "No use for him to wash when even his name means bad smell! He is a white man. That is why he smells bad. All white men smell bad."

Quanah scowled at them. "I am Comanche," he shouted. "My father is Peta Nocona, great war chief of the Comanches."

"Your mother is of the white man's people," Bear Tail called. "Can you say that is not true?"

Quanah didn't answer. He knew that his mother, Naudah, was indeed white. Captured by the

Comanches when she was only nine, Cynthia Ann Parker soon forgot her family. She took the Indian name Naudah and lived happily with the Comanches. In time she married a chief and had a baby named Quanah.

Quanah loved his mother dearly, but he wished that the other boys would not tease him. Quickly he ducked his whole body beneath the cold water. Perhaps that would wash away the smell.

The Llano River was close to a great level grassland called the Staked Plains in what is now western Texas. Many buffalo grazed on the rich grass. The Indians said there were as many buffalo as there were leaves on the trees or stars in the sky.

Tribes who made their homes on these rolling plains were called Plains Indians. Among them were many bands of Comanches.

The Comanches did not always stay in one place. They followed the buffalo herds north across the plains in summer, south in winter. Buffalo meat was their chief food. They made the shaggy black hides into bed robes, lodges, and clothing. They made the horns into cups and spoons, and the bones into tools. The sinew was made into bowstrings and thread. Even the hoofs could be boiled into glue. Quanah's people could not live without the great humpbacked creatures.

Now Quanah climbed from the river and put on his breech clout and moccasins. Then he went to the circle of lodges.

His mother was cooking. She put a slice of meat on a long green stick and hung it over the fire. His small brother, Pecos, was playing with some pebbles.

"You did not swim long, my son," his mother said.

"I will not swim with those who call me white man," Quanah said scornfully.

Quanah's mother smiled at the boy's angry face, but her bright blue eyes looked sad.

"You are Comanche," she said. "Pay no attention if the others tease you. It is only boys' talk. They will forget."

Quanah thought about Naudah's words. Then he nodded. "A-ya. Yes. I will do as my mother says. I will be such. a good Comanche that soon they will not want to tease."

That night Quanah told his father, "I want a big bow and some arrows. I shall be a great warrior."

"The buffalo will run away when they see such a great warrior coming," his father smiled. "How then will we get any meat?"

But Chief Peta Nocona had a light bow and some arrows made for his little son and gave him a pony for his own.

2. The Buffalo Hunt

Like all Comanche boys, Quanah began to be "grown up" when he was twelve. He worked hard to learn the things a Comanche warrior must know. As time passed everyone forgot that he was half-white.

He learned to shoot an arrow straight to its target and to hurl a lance. He learned to swim and to run fast and long.

He could live off the land, finding nuts and berries to eat when he was hungry, and water holes to drink from when he was thirsty.

He could trail an animal or an enemy. He could imitate the hoot of an owl, the gobble of a wild turkey, and the howl of a wolf.

He learned the Indian sign language, and how to send smoke signals. He knew how to stop the bleeding from an arrow or bullet wound.

He could ride a pony and hang from its side or crawl under its belly when it was racing like the wind. He could rope wild horses. He could make sharp bone lances and straight arrows. At last he was old enough to go on a hunt with his father and the other men in the tribe.

The night before the hunt Quanah was too excited to sleep. He lay awake upon his bed of buffalo

robes and told himself all the things his father had
said he must remember tomorrow:

> Go quietly. Do not talk. Make no noise.
> Buffalo are easily frightened and if they
> stampede we will lose our winter meat.
> Do not ride ahead of the others. Wait
> until the hunt leader gives the signal,
> then ride fast into the herd and begin
> shooting. Watch out for any wounded
> animals. They will charge a rider. Re-
> member that buffalo hunting is no boys'
> game. It is serious and dangerous busi-
> ness. Hunters who break the rules are
> not allowed to hunt again for a long
> time.

"I shall not break the rules," Quanah promised
the silvery moon that peeped into the lodge through
the open space at the doorway.

Soon it was dawn, and time to go. Like all the
hunters, Quanah wore only a breech clout and moccasins. Too many clothes would get in the way.

Quanah's heart was thumping with excitement, but
he rode quietly and kept his eyes on the leader.
Suddenly the man raised his hand over his head,
then dropped it to his side. That was the signal.
Quanah kicked his pony into a run. Pell-mell he

In his first buffalo hunt, Quanah used all the skills he had learned.

raced straight into the heart of the great herd. Then all at once he was afraid!

Dust swirled around him, and there was a vast confusion of noise and action. Men shouted. Horses reared. Buffalo plunged right and left in a desperate effort to escape the hunters. Quanah heard the sharp snap of bowstrings and the maddened bellowing of a cow for her calf. He saw dying animals stagger and fall to the ground. For a moment he wanted to run away. Then he shook himself angrily, and his fear passed.

Carefully he fitted an arrow to his bow. Stretching far forward over his pony's head, he aimed at a large buffalo.

How true his arrow sped! It went straight to the chest and through the heart. The big beast dropped to its knees, then to the ground, and lay still.

"Well done, son," said a pleased voice.

Quanah turned to find Chief Peta Nocona riding behind him. He had not known his father was so near, but he was glad that his father had seen the good shot. He did not suspect that the chief had been keeping watch over his son's safety. Peta Nocona remembered his own first hunt and how easy it was for an inexperienced boy to be frightened.

His father cut the tongue from Quanah's first kill. The tongue was the best part of the meat. "Give it to an old man too weak to hunt anymore," Peta Nocona said. Quanah knew that this was a Comanche custom to teach the young to be kind to old people.

That evening at the feast, Quanah did not eat any of the meat from his buffalo. This was a Comanche custom to teach the young not to be greedy.

Happily he watched the others feasting on his kill. Even his new baby sister, Prairie Flower, was sucking on a bone.

"Now I am a hunter," he thought proudly. "Now I shall bring much meat to my mother's cooking fire."

3. Day of Sorrow

Soon the days grew short and the nights cold. It was time for Quanah's people to move to a winter camp.

The Comanches were called a nomadic people because, like all wandering nomads who have no fixed home, they moved so often. It was easy for them to leave one camp and set up another. They had no furniture to carry, only their soft buffalo-hide beds. They had their clothing, small articles such as bowls made from the wood of elm or oak trees, tools of stone or bone, weapons, and pipes.

When Chief Peta Nocona gave the order to move, everyone became very busy.

The men rounded up the pony herd. The women wrapped their belongings in animal skins and packed them on horses or in travois. Travois were crude baskets fastened upon two long poles which were tied to a horse's saddle. The other ends of the poles dragged on the ground. Each buffalo-hide lodge was rolled and packed on a horse, and the stout poles that held up the lodge were tied to the pack saddle and left to drag behind the horse.

In a few hours the band was ready to seek a new camp.

Chief Nocona led them far south to a spot near

the beautiful cliffs of the Pease River. The Indians called it Prairie Dog Town River because so many of the furry little animals dug their burrows on the nearby plains.

"A-ya. This is a good place," said the Chief. "There is dry grass for our horses and plenty of wood for our campfires."

They unpacked their bundles. They set up their lodges with every door flap facing the east and the rising sun. They dug pits for their fires. They turned their pony herds out to graze. Now they were ready for winter.

But soon there was sadness in the camp. Quanah's people sang the death song because white soldiers were attacking nearby Indian villages and burning the lodges. They were United States Cavalry troops sent to punish the Indians for raiding white settlements.

Chief Nocona led his warriors out to avenge their Indian friends. Quanah was still too young to go on a war party.

"Someday I will be old enough," he thought. "I will ride to war beside my father. I will take many scalps and drive the white man from our land."

One day the blue-coated soldiers attacked Quanah's camp. They rode in from two sides and shot many guns. Women and children ran from the lodges in terror and tried to hide. Warriors grabbed their bows and arrows.

Quanah and his younger brother, Pecos, ran to a nearby creek. They hid in the bushes and listened to the guns. Anger and sorrow filled Quanah's heart.

"Arrows are no good against guns," he whispered bitterly to Pecos.

The battle did not last long. When it ended, Peta Nocona's band had been wiped out. The brave chief was dead.

Naudah was taken captive because the soldiers saw her blue eyes. They knew she was a white woman, and they intended to return her to her people. They took Prairie Flower, too.

The soldiers destroyed every lodge. Then a blizzard came, and the soldiers left.

Quanah and Pecos crept from their hiding place. Icy sleet whipped their faces. The storm was like a white blanket around them. The frightened, freezing boys found that their home and parents were gone. They were alone on the prairie.

"Let us walk," Quanah said. "We will not feel so cold if we keep walking."

At last through the storm Quanah's keen eyes saw some dim moving figures. His sharp ears heard a voice. "*Kee-mah!*" it called. "Come!"

It was Horseback who called. He was chief of a

Chief Horseback's camp. The old Comanche warrior took Quanah and his brother here.

neighboring band and a ferocious warrior. He was looking for any who had escaped the soldiers.

He took the boys to his camp. A few days later he sent Pecos to another Comanche village where there was a family with no sons. Quanah stayed with Horseback and lived in Horseback's lodge.

The half-white boy grew to manhood in Horseback's camp. He rode beside the old chief on many raids against the whites. They burned homes, stole livestock, and took scalps. Quanah was an even more savage warrior than Horseback. He could never forget what the hated white man had done to his family.

"Even Pecos is dead," he thought bitterly. "He grew sick and died in a strange village among strangers. For that, too, I will make the white man pay."

From southern Texas to Kansas, no white settlement was safe from Horseback and Quanah.

When Quanah was eighteen years old, he organized his own band of Comanches. They were called the Quahadas. Many young braves with their wives and children joined his band. They knew Quanah was a courageous and skillful leader. When they saw he wore an eagle claw hung from a thong around his neck, the braves called him "Quanah, Eagle of the Comanches."

The Comanches were the most hostile and fierce Indians on the plains. Soon the Quahadas were the fiercest of all.

One summer day a scout brought news to Quanah. Quanah called his warriors together.

"The white chiefs want to make peace with the Indians," he said. "They have invited all the southern tribes to a big council meeting. They will sign a peace treaty with us and give us presents. Shall we go?"

Big Deer spoke up. "I do not trust their treaties.

Many tribes have signed treaty papers. But the papers say one thing, and the white man does another. Treaties are papers that talk two ways."

"That is so," agreed Red Leaf. "The white man talks with a crooked tongue. Still it would be wise to go and hear what he is saying now, and I would like to have a present."

They all looked at Quanah. He was the leader. He must decide.

Slowly Quanah began to speak:

"It will be a big powwow. There will be many great tribal chiefs there. I have heard their names and deeds. Let those of you who wish, go with me to see these great warriors. Let us take the white man's presents. Let us hear his words and learn if it is peace he wants, or more of our land."

4. To the Powwow

For many days Quanah and his party rode north through the Staked Plains to the meeting place.

It was the end of summer, 1867. Wild grapes were ripe. Leaves of the cottonwood trees were turning yellow. The young brave looked at his beautiful land with sad eyes. How much longer would it be Indian land, he wondered. More and more white men were moving in.

"They come like ants in a steady stream," he thought. And now he had heard they were building a big iron horse that raced across the plains and never grew tired. White men called it a railroad train.

At last the party came to Medicine Lodge Valley, where the council was to meet. It was in Kansas on a little branch of the Arkansas River.

Quanah stared in surprise.

"*Cah-bogn!* Look!" he exclaimed to Red Leaf who rode beside him. "This is an even bigger powwow than I thought!"

A thousand Indian lodges were set up for miles along the pleasant stream. To one side the tents of the white soldiers stood in long neat rows. Huge herds of ponies grazed on nearby hills.

Slowly Quanah rode through the encampment. He saw 30 covered wagons filled with white-man goods. He saw big stacks of presents for the Indians. There were beads and bracelets and useful things like cooking pots, knives, and axes. There were blankets, brown sugar, and tobacco. There were mirrors, paint, saddles, and bridles.

Best of all, he saw the great chiefs of his people.

Among the Comanches were Painted Lips and the wise old chief, Ten Bears.

In the Apache camp, Crow and Iron Shirt were

pointed out to him. In the Arapaho camp there were Spotted Wolf and Little Raven. At the Cheyenne camp were Black Kettle and Bull Bear. The famous Satanta was in the Kiowa camp, and also Kicking Bird.

Five thousand Plains Indians had traveled to Medicine Lodge, and many white people. Quanah was excited at seeing such a large gathering.

"Perhaps there will be peace after all," he told Red Leaf hopefully.

But when the meeting began, he lost hope.

As he listened to the white leaders' words, he began to understand a sad thing. White men did not think they were doing wrong by taking the Indians' land. They thought it was right to plow fields and build houses in the Staked Plains!

"We want to bring civilization to this wilderness," said N. G. Taylor, the Commissioner of Indian Affairs. He had been sent there by the Great White Father in Washington, D.C.

Commissioner Taylor said the Indians did not need such a vast land. They used it only to hunt. He said the Indians should move to reservations set up for them by the United States government.

"There you will be fed and cared for," he said. "You won't need to hunt any more."

Other whites made speeches to the red men. They

said: "You must not kill any more white people or steal their cattle and horses. You must not tear up the tracks of the new railroad. You must learn the ways of the reservation and obey the rules. Then everyone can live in peace."

"Peace!" Quanah spat out the word to Red Leaf as though it had a bad taste. "What kind of peace is it if the Indian must live only where the white man puts him and do only what the white man says?"

Many tribal chiefs spoke against the reservation plan. Wrinkled old Ten Bears spoke for the Comanches.

At Medicine Lodge Valley, thousands of Plains Indians gathered to hear the White Father's words.

"There has been trouble, but it was not begun by us," he told the white people. "It was you who sent out the first soldier and we who sent the second.

"The blue-dressed soldiers came from out of the night when it was dark and still, and for campfires they lit our lodges.

"You say you want to put us on reservations, to build us houses. I do not want them. I was born on the prairie, where the wind blew free and there was nothing to break the light of the sun. I was born where there were no enclosures and where everything drew a free breath.

"I want to die there, and not within walls."

"A-ya. Yes," said the listening Quanah. "We were born free, and we must die free."

But the white men paid no attention to Ten Bears. They said the treaty must be signed, or else the soldiers would wipe out every Indian village.

Most of the tribal chiefs signed for their people. They were afraid not to sign. But others refused, among them many Comanches.

Quanah said scornfully: "My band is not going to live on a reservation. Tell the white chiefs that the Quahadas are warriors and will surrender when the blue-coats whip us on the Staked Plains."

Then he mounted his pony and rode angrily away. He didn't wait to get his present.

5. Quanah Calls a War Council

It was time for a hunt. The Quahadas needed fresh meat. Their winter supply of dried buffalo meat was nearly gone.

Quanah sent his scouts to find the buffalo herds that returned to the Staked Plains each spring.

When the scouts came back they said: "There are no buffalo herds. We rode for many sleeps but found only a few small bunches, not enough meat to feed us more than a little while. The great herds are gone."

Quanah's heart grew heavy at their sad words.

Seven springs had passed since the Medicine Lodge Council. The blue-coats had not whipped the Quahadas, but a worse thing had happened.

White hunters with powerful guns had moved onto the plains. They had killed tens of thousands of buffalo. They could sell the thick hides for good prices. They did not want the meat. They left the skinned buffalo to rot on the prairie, food for only wolves and coyotes.

"This is bad trouble," Quanah said.

He looked around his busy camp and wondered how he could tell his people of the hungry days ahead. Many women were working before their lodges. Some sewed clothing from animal skins while others painted moccasin designs with earth colors or tended cooking fires. Children played nearby. Old people sat in the soft spring sunshine and talked of long-ago hunts and battles.

Quanah's face grew sad and sadder still as he watched some braves carefully fitting hawk feathers to new arrows. They were getting ready to go after buffalo. How could he tell them that they didn't need the arrows now that the buffalo were gone?

Last of all Quanah looked toward his own lodge. He knew that inside was his wife, Weckeah, and his young children. He had married Weckeah, daughter of Chief Yellow Bear, three years ago. He remembered how, to show his respect for Weckeah, he had given Yellow Bear seventeen ponies. How could he tell Weckeah that soon there would be no food for the children?

Isa-tai was the Quahada medicine man. He was believed to be very wise and to know the ways of magic. He painted his pony with a yellow "medicine" paint that he said would make bullets bounce off. When he heard the scouts' report he told Quanah, "We must drive the hunters away. The Great Spirit has told me that when they are gone the buffalo will come back."

"Such a battle would take many warriors," Quanah said doubtfully.

"Call a war council of all the tribes. Make a big war plan," Isa-tai advised. "There is no other way to bring back the buffalo."

So again Quanah sent out his scouts. They carried the war message to all the free bands left on the plains.

Soon the chiefs from many camps came to meet with Quanah, for in some camps the people were already beginning to suffer. They heard Isa-tai's words that the Great Spirit promised them victory if they fought the hide hunters.

"There are many hide hunters at a place far from here called Adobe Walls. We must destroy them," said Isa-tai. "Then the buffalo will come back."

"We need the buffalo back," said the chiefs. "The faces of our wives and children grow thin for want of meat."

Quanah filled his war pipe. He offered the first puff of smoke to the sun, the second to the earth, the next to the four winds. Then he sent the pipe around the circle of chiefs.

The chiefs returned to their camps to make ready. The braves sharpened their lances. They feathered arrows. Those who had guns cleaned them well. Isa-tai painted his pony yellow from head to tail. They danced the war dance. At last it was time to be on their way.

A Comanche war party rides off to battle.

One evening in June 1874, 700 warriors met not far from Adobe Walls. They were the largest war party ever gathered on the Staked Plains to fight the whites. They wore war paint and feathers. They carried shields of dried buffalo hide. They had lances and clubs, many arrows, and some guns. Best of all, they thought, they had Isa-tai's magic.

"We will surprise the hunters at dawn and attack them while they sleep," Quanah said. "Isa-tai promises to make strong medicine to help us."

110

They rode swiftly and silently through the summer night toward Adobe Walls. Their hopes were high. Tomorrow they would win a victory and bring back the buffalo. Life would be good again.

6. Battle at Adobe Walls

Adobe Walls was a log camp and trading post for buffalo hunters in north Texas. There were several large cabins with strong log walls and roofs made of poles covered with earth. Atop the buildings were protected lookout posts. There was a horse corral, and nearby ran a good-sized creek.

Twenty-eight white hunters were asleep at the post that June night. Two white traders slept in their wagon outside the gate of the corral. They were the only men at Adobe Walls. Their sleep was peaceful, for they did not know that hundreds of war-painted Indians were nearby.

Then a strange thing happened at the post. In the middle of the night a pole holding the roof of one of the buildings broke.

The loud noise awoke the men. They shouted to one another: "Get up! Everybody get up! We must brace the roof or it will fall!" It was almost daylight before they finished the work—much too late to go back to bed.

Young Billy Dixon went outside for his horse, which was staked by the creek. Quanah was hiding in the woods beyond the creek. He watched the hunter untie the horse. Back among the trees the warriors waited for the signal to attack.

The first pink streaks of dawn lighted the sky. Birds began to sing. Suddenly Quanah saw the hunter stare into the woods, as though he had seen something move. Then the man reached quickly for his rifle.

Quanah knew they were discovered. The surprise attack was spoiled.

"*Kee-mah!* Come!" he shouted to his warriors.

With angry yells they charged out of the woods, straight at the hunter. He raised his gun and fired a shot to warn his friends. Then he jumped on his horse and raced for the post while arrows zipped around him.

He made it safely, but the braves killed and scalped the two traders sleeping in their wagon and stampeded their horses in the corral. From the cabins the wide-awake hunters sent a shower of bullets into the red ranks.

War whoops and gunfire, dust and smoke filled the morning air. The first charge of the Indians carried them right up to the buildings. They beat on the barred doors and windows with club and lance.

Some warriors backed their horses violently against the doors and tried to break them in. The reply of the hunters was deadly, and Adobe, Walls blazed in the roar of their heavy guns.

Many braves fell in the first charge. The others sent their arrows whizzing through the air only to stick harmlessly in the thick walls.

Again and again the Indians charged. The rising sun gleamed red on their painted faces and tousled feathers. They were beaten back by guns that could drop a 2,000-pound buffalo with one shot from 600 yards away.

The men in the cabins were some of the finest marksmen in the world. Their guns were powerful rifles known as the Sharps "Big 50" or "Buffalo Gun." People said it was "packaged thunder and lightning" that was almost too much gun for any man. Many Indians had only bows and arrows. Some had "trade" guns that would not shoot far.

Quanah fought bravely. His pony was killed, and he found another. He was wounded but kept fighting.

The battle lasted three days. Many braves were killed, but only one hunter. The hunters stayed safe behind their sturdy walls. Since this was a trading post, they had plenty of food and ammunition. There were no portholes in the cabins from which to fire their guns, but through cracks in the logs and from the lookout posts, they sprayed death on the red men.

On the third afternoon some Comanches sat talking atop a bluff. Suddenly one toppled from his pony. He had been killed by a shot from the post —nearly a mile away!

"We cannot fight such guns," Quanah said. "They have won the battle."

Sadly the other chiefs agreed. "The white man's gun travels too far," they said. "His gun shoots today and kills tomorrow."

With heavy heart Quanah led his warriors down the long road home. The sorrowing Comanches did not know that Adobe Walls was their last battle. Never again would they smoke the war pipe and ride out to fight for their land and their people.

7. Hunger on the Plains

Quanah stood outside his lodge and looked up at the sky. There was not a cloud anywhere. The sky was like a hot blue roof over the Staked Plains.

He turned to Isa-tai. "Use your medicine to make rain," he said. Isa-tai only looked troubled and walked away.

It had been two moons since the defeat at Adobe Walls. Summer was almost gone. It was the hottest, driest summer Quanah had ever known. Water holes and streams dried up for lack of rain. The grass was like hay. There were deep cracks in the sun-baked earth. The people were suffering.

A party of Comanches and their families rode into the Quahada camp. Quanah saw his old friend High Buffalo of the Nokonis band. He welcomed him.

"The words I must speak are bitter as gourds in my mouth," High Buffalo said. "I am taking my people to the reservation. We will surrender."

Quanah was greatly surprised.

"We have no choice," explained High Buffalo. "Word has come from the white men that every warrior must go to his reservation and stay there. He must answer roll call every day. The white men are angry because we fought at Adobe Walls. They are sending their soldiers to find and kill every Indian not on the reservation."

"They won't find me," Quanah said. "We will camp far away. There is no water, and the blue-coats' horses will die on the trail. Their horses are not used to hardships like our ponies. If the soldiers do come near, we will go farther away. They will tire trying to find us."

"They will find you, my friend," High Buffalo said. "There is no place left to hide. And the buffalo are gone." He led his band away.

In the fall the rains came, but now there was too much water. The rains were like floods. Streams overflowed their banks, and the ground turned to mud. There were few berries and nuts to eat, and no meat.

The white soldiers were always near. They drove the weary Indians before them like rabbits.

Each time Quanah's people set up a new camp, his scouts brought word that the soldiers were coming again. The Quahadas did not have time to pack all their goods and round up their pony herds. They had to leave much goods and many ponies behind.

In time they lost almost everything: their clothes and lodges and even their cooking pots.

Winter came, and it was bitterly cold. There was no food. A hunter must have his horse and weapons even to hunt a deer, and many of these had been left behind on the long hard marches. The people were always hungry. Many grew sick.

Quanah's scouts brought news that Stone Calf had surrendered his band. Then the other chiefs surrendered—Lone Wolf, Red Otter, Swan, and Poor Buffalo, then Red Foot and White Wolf.

Soon the Quahadas were the only free Indians left on the plains.

One day Quanah walked to a sandy hill near his camp. He sat on a rock and drew his robe over his head as a sign of sorrow. He tried to think what to do.

His people were free hunters and warriors. Should he lead them to a reservation where they must dig in the fields? Their children would then grow up in the white man's ways. His own children—what of them? Would they forget the old ways of their ancestors?

But High Buffalo had surrendered and so had Lone Wolf and Stone Calf.

"If I do not surrender, the children and the old and sick will die," Quanah thought. "They need food and care."

"I am a warrior," Quanah told himself. "I would rather die fighting than surrender, but I cannot choose for myself. I must choose for my people."

He pulled the blanket from his head and walked back to camp. His step was firm, for he had chosen.

"*Kee-mah!* Come!" he shouted to the Quahadas. "Everybody get ready. Today we must travel a new road."

"What road?" asked a brave.

"The white man's road," Quanah said.

And so in the spring of 1875, the Quahadas started the long journey to the Comanche reservation in western Oklahoma. They were the last band of Comanches to surrender to the white men.

This photograph of Quanah was taken after some fifteen years on the reservation. He was one of the few fighting chiefs who adjusted to reservation life and succeeded on the "white man's road."

8. The Peacemaker

Swiftly the years sped by. Quanah was so busy that he scarcely noticed their passing. The same intelligence and energy that had made him a Quahada chief when he was an eighteen-year-old orphan on the plains now made him a leader in his new life.

He tried to teach his people to accept the new ways and be friends with the white man. It was their only chance to be happy again, he knew. The buffalo were gone, the plains empty. The red man had no choice now but to walk the white man's road.

Quanah took a step on that road when he added his mother's last name to his own. He was known after this as Quanah Parker.

He was appointed principal chief of all the Comanches. Under his leadership the Comanches prospered. Then men from the Kiowa and other tribes came to Quanah's lodge for advice. Soon his word carried power at many council fires.

To the nation Quanah came to represent not only the Comanche cause but that of all Indians. Leaders from many tribes visited the Comanche reservation to powwow—even the fierce Apache fighter, Geronimo. White men came to see Quanah too. Quanah himself traveled to Washington, D.C., many times on behalf of the Indians.

Quanah (far left) led this delegation of Indians to
Washington in the 1890s on tribal business.

"We are one people," Quanah often said. "We
must walk the peace road together."

Quanah lived to be an old man, loved and honored
by all. He died at his home on a bright February
day in 1911. Many newspapers wrote about him, saying the whole nation mourned him and that the
respect in which he was held had helped all Indians.

Two thousand white and red men went to his
funeral. Speakers told what a great man he was.

Today all over the American Southwest people remember Quanah Parker and name towns, streets, schools, and parks after him. The United States Congress voted money for a fine monument for his grave. The tall red shaft stands in the heart of the land he loved, where fresh winds stir the prairie grass and sometimes a hawk wheels overhead.

The words carved on the monument say:

RESTING HERE UNTIL THE DAY BREAKS

AND THE SHADOWS FALL

AND DARKNESS DISAPPEARS

IS QUANAH PARKER,

THE LAST CHIEF OF THE COMANCHES.

In the Words of Quanah

To the old Comanche chiefs, after the signing of the Medicine Lodge Treaty:

"You have taken your scalps and won honor as warriors. You have many ponies, and it pleases you to have the gifts and rations of the white men. We too want to win honors. I am glad that they did not ask me to sign the treaty. I am not going to a reservation. The Quahadas are free. . . . Now I am going to them, and we shall live just as we have always lived. Tell the white chiefs, when they ask, that the Quahadas are warriors and that we are not afraid."

To the young braves, on the Comanche reservation in Oklahoma:

"If you were going to a strange place to make war, you would not hold back. You are going to bring back goods that the agent will give out to the whole tribe, instead of war plunder. . . . You will not fight, to kill men, but you will have hardships and work to undergo. That takes strong, brave men."

About Quanah's People

The Comanches were Plains Indians who lived in the Southwest. Like other tribes who roamed the plains, the Comanches were fierce warriors and hunters of buffalo. They were especially known for their skill in capturing and training wild mustangs. Few other Indians could equal them in horsemanship. The map below shows the Staked Plains of western Texas and New Mexico, where the Comanches wandered in search of buffalo; Medicine Lodge Valley, where many Comanches refused to sign a treaty with the whites; and Adobe Walls, where Quanah's band fought their last battle.

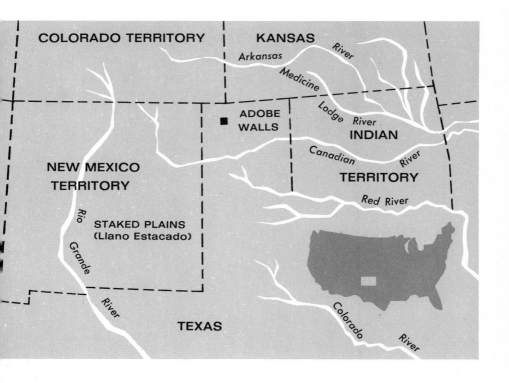

Chief Joseph

Guardian of the Nez Perces

by Elizabeth Rider Montgomery

Chief Joseph tried to keep peace with the white
man even after his band of Nez Perces were
driven out of the beautiful Wallowa Valley, their
ancestral home. But Indians and white men
clashed, and Joseph's people set out on the
remarkable 1,000-mile flight from the army that
took them almost to Canada and safety.

125

1. No More Mission School

Young Joseph showed his neat printing to his little brother.

"See this, Ollokot," he said proudly. "These are Nez Perce words. I will show you how to print them."

In the little schoolroom, the two small Indian boys bent over their papers. As they worked, they read aloud in Nez Perce, "Our Father, Who Art in Heaven. . . ." All around them other Indians said their lessons aloud, too.

It was the year 1847, in what is now western Idaho. Joseph and Ollokot were the sons of Tu-eka-kas, a wealthy Nez Perce chief. The boys attended the Presbyterian mission school at Lapwai, run by Mr. and Mrs. Spalding. These missionaries were teaching Nez Perces to read and write. They wanted the Indians to become Christians. They also wanted them to be farmers so they would settle down in one place.

Mrs. Spalding came to look at Joseph's work. "That is fine, Joseph," she said. "Ollokot is doing well, too. Soon you can both read your father's Bible."

Joseph had often seen his father's "Bible," the Gospel of Matthew printed in Nez Perce. The chief was very proud of it.

Now Mrs. Spalding smiled down at earnest Joseph and laughing Ollokot.

"Your father is a true Christian," she told them. "He is a fine man and a good chief."

The schoolroom door opened. Chief Tu-eka-kas, tall and proud, stalked in.

"Come, my sons," the chief roared. "We are returning to Wallowa."

"Oh, no!" protested Mrs. Spalding. "Do not take the boys out of school."

"A white man put shame on me," the chief announced. "He gave me a worn-out blanket." A government man, who was passing out blankets to Indians, had given Chief Tu-eka-kas a blanket with holes.

"I am not a poor man," Tu-eka-kas stormed. "I need no such gift."

In spite of everything Mrs. Spalding said, the chief took Joseph and Ollokot out of school.

The people of Tu-eka-kas's band had set up their village near the mission buildings. Now they all began to pack. Joseph's sisters helped their mother,

Arenoth, take down the tepees and roll the buffalo-skin coverings. They helped her tie the lodge poles into bundles. They packed the family's blankets, the tightly coiled baskets used for cooking, their wooden eating bowls, and their horn spoons.

Joseph and Ollokot gathered up the fishing gear, while their older brother, Sousouquee, helped men round up horses and cattle. Then the Wallowa band of Nez Perces left the Lapwai mission. Joseph rode up front by his father and his brothers. His school days were over. His father would never forgive the white people for insulting him.

2. Boyhood in Wallowa

In Wallowa Valley Joseph soon forgot most of what he had learned. His days were busy and happy.

Wallowa, in eastern Oregon, was the beloved summer home of Tu-eka-kas's people. All the other Nez Perce bands agreed that the valley belonged to them. High mountains guarded the valley. The lake and rivers were full of fish. Every morning when the sun rose over the mountains, the village crier rode among the lodges shouting:

"I wonder if everyone is up! It is morning. Rise up! Go see to the horses, lest a wolf has killed one. Thanks be that we are alive!"

Tu-eka-kas was chief of the Nez Perces and the father of Joseph and Ollokot.

Joseph Taawiatakhis.
Chief of the Nez percé Indians

Arenoth came from the tepee to stir the fire. Joseph and Ollokot came out too. They bathed in the river.

After breakfast the boys got on their horses. The Nez Perces raised very fine horses. Even the smallest children were good horsemen. With other Nez Perce boys, Joseph raced along the lake shore. He was learning to hang on one side of his horse while shooting an arrow from under the horse's neck.

When they tired of racing, Joseph and his brother came back to the village. They watched Arenoth cook camas roots in pits lined with stones and roast salmon and venison over open fires. They saw their sisters scraping deer hides, which would be used to make clothing.

The little boys watched their father's skillful work on a new bow made from a mountain sheep's horn. They watched Sousouquee and other young warriors decorate war bonnets with eagle feathers.

"Someday I shall wear a war bonnet," Ollokot said. "I will be a brave warrior."

"I shall be a chief," said Joseph. "I shall take care of my people."

In the evenings the Indians gathered around fires in the longhouse. This was a large building 150 feet long. The roof was covered with cattail mats. Down the center was a row of fires.

Joseph enjoyed these evenings. Old men repeated stories and myths, teaching the children tribal history and legend.

One man told about the coming of the Lewis and Clark expedition to Nez Perce country. The Nez Perces promised to keep peace with the white people forever.

"Our people have never broken that promise," Tu-eka-kas told his sons.

A storyteller told about the coming of the missionaries. Another explained how some French trappers named the tribe "Nez Perce," or "Pierced Nose," because some men wore nose ornaments.

Although they had heard these stories over and over again, Joseph and Ollokot always listened eagerly.

Other Indians told the young children about their tribe. "Our Nez Perce nation has a number of bands," they said. "Each band has it own village, its own fishing and hunting grounds, and its own chief. Village council meetings are held with chief and headman. Tribal councils are held with the chiefs of different bands. In any Nez Perce council, all must agree, or there is no decision. A chief can speak only for his own band."

Sometimes men spoke of the greatness of the Nez Perce nation. "We are the biggest, the richest, and the strongest Indian tribe in this land," they said proudly. "Our beautiful Appaloosa horses are famous. We raise excellent cattle, too, and we have miles and miles of grazing land."

Joseph's eyes shone as he listened. How proud he was to be a Nez Perce!

3. The Sacred Vigil

The happy seasons passed. Joseph's father taught him to hunt, to fish, and to make spears, knives, and arrows. He taught him to imitate the calls of birds and animals.

Joseph learned the Indian Spirit Laws too. He learned that the Great Spirit sees and hears everything. Joseph understood that he must treat others the way he wanted to be treated. He learned that lying is the very worst sin, especially if the lie is told three times.

When Joseph was about thirteen, Chief Tu-eka-kas said to him, "It is time to keep your sacred vigil, my son."

Very early the next morning, Joseph prepared for his vigil. Naked, unarmed, he left the village and the valley. Up, up into the mountains he climbed. At last he reached the top of a ridge, where he built a little heap of stones.

Far below him, Joseph could see Lake Wallowa and the big valley. The village on the lake shore looked very tiny. The boy closed his eyes and began to pray. He prayed to the Christian God and to the Indians' Great Spirit. Sometimes he thought that they were the same God.

For hours Joseph prayed and waited, but no guardian spirit came. When night fell he made a little fire to keep from freezing. He could hear animals moving nearby, but he was not afraid. Nothing would hurt a young Indian keeping the sacred vigil. His eyes grew heavy, but he would not sleep.

The night dragged on. Daylight came. Joseph was hungry, but he would not think about food. He was very thirsty, but he would not think about water. He kept on praying.

As the day passed, Joseph began to feel light-headed. That night a storm came up. Wind blew, rain fell, lightning flashed, and thunder rolled.

Finally Joseph could not keep his eyes open. In spite of the noise of the storm, he lay on the ground and slept. While he was sleeping, Joseph had a vivid dream.

On a loud roll of thunder, a man seemed to float in the air. A blanket trailed behind him. With each crash of thunder, the blanket leaped and waved.

"My boy," said the dream figure, "look at me. I am Thunder. I will give you my power, if you always do what I tell you."

The dream figure, Thunder, then taught Joseph a song and a dance that would be his alone throughout his life.

When Joseph woke he said joyfully, "Thunder is my guardian spirit." He knew that this was a very fine omen, or sign, for the things that live in the sky are powerful guardian spirits.

Joseph returned to his village. "The Great Spirit

was good to me," he told his father. Joseph bathed, and then his mother brought him food. He lay down on a grass bed in the tepee and fell fast asleep.

Several moons later the Guardian Spirit Dance was held for those who had kept the sacred vigil. Joseph dressed carefully for it. His deerskin shirt and leggings had been cleaned with white clay from the lake shore. He put on his finest moccasins and hung many strings of beads around his neck. He wove narrow strips of fur into his long braids. He painted his face with red and yellow paint. Then he threw his richest blanket around his shoulders.

The Dance of the Guardian Spirit was held in the longhouse. Soon it was Joseph's turn to perform. He stepped into the light of the flickering fires. Joseph sang his special song and shuffled his feet in his dance. He made motions with his hands, his arms, his entire body. His blanket leaped and waved to show that Thunder was his guardian spirit.

Other Indians began to sing with Joseph. By the time he finished his dance, everybody was singing with him.

"Him-mut-too-yah-lat-kekt," they sang. "Joseph's name is now Thunder-Rolling-in-the-Mountains."

"It is a good name," the old men said approvingly.

Joseph smiled happily.

4. The Great Council

Tu-eka-kas knew that his sons should learn about the responsibilities of a Nez Perce chief. He often called them from their games to sit beside him. They listened as he decided disputes among families. They saw how he kept thoughtless young men under control. They learned that a chief had no power to force his people to obey. He ruled by convincing them that his advice was wise and his decisions just.

Many white men were coming to the Indians' land now. They came over a road called the Oregon Trail. Nez Perce men sometimes went to meet them and trade horses for cattle.

A few white people came to Wallowa Valley and built homes and made farms. At first the Indians did not object.

"There is plenty of room here for all," Tu-eka-kas told his people.

Soon, however, many of the white settlers seemed to think that they owned Wallowa Valley. They took more and more land. Quarrels arose between the white men and the Indians.

When Joseph was fifteen, Governor Stevens, the new white governor in the Northwest, invited all Indian tribes to a council in the Walla Walla Valley.

Sousouquee, Joseph, and Ollokot went to the council

with Tu-eka-kas. Of the 5,000 Indians who attended, half were Nez Perces. They set up their tepees by the river.

The council met near the governor's tent. The governor sat on a bench, while the Indians gathered around him. Tu-eka-kas and other chiefs sat in front with their sub-chiefs behind them. Joseph and Ollokot stood in the background.

"I will open my heart to you," Governor Stevens said. "I speak for our president in Washington. He sends you greetings. He loves the Indians as if they were his own children. He wants to help you."

At the meeting at Walla Walla, an artist painted the Nez Perces parading proudly on horseback.

Joseph wondered what the president could do for his people that they could not do for themselves. "Many white men have come west to build houses and make farms. If Indians and white people are to live in peace, the Indians must have reservations, or land set aside for them."

Those words puzzled Joseph. Wouldn't it be simpler and fairer to keep white men out of Indian country?

Governor Stevens explained his plan. The Nez Perce reservation would include Wallowa Valley and Lapwai, and the Indians would be paid for the land they gave up. Schools and sawmills would be built. Indians would be given tools, clothes, and money.

Many Indian chiefs objected.

"The Earth Mother is for all men," Chief Tu-eka-kas argued. "No man owns her. No man can buy her. None can sell her."

Joseph nodded. His father spoke the truth. But Governor Stevens did not listen to the wise words of Chief Tu-eka-kas.

The council continued for many days. Each day the Indians listened to the governor. Each evening they spent in their villages. Joseph and Ollokot joined in the horse races and games with other Nez Perce boys. Ollokot won many of the races, and Joseph was proud of his brother.

One evening Joseph went to the council fire where all the men were discussing the governor's plan. Some of the young men wanted to fight to keep their homeland. Older men counseled peace.

"Indians can never win a war against white armies," Tu-eka-kas said. "In all the seasons the white man has been pushing westward, Indians have never won a war."

So on June 11, 1855, Tu-eka-kas put his mark on Governor Stevens's treaty.

When they returned to Wallowa, Tu-eka-kas said, "We will plant poles around our valley." Joseph and Ollokot helped mark part of the Nez Perce reservation with tall poles.

"Now," said their father, "white people will know this is Nez Perce land."

"My father is very wise," thought Joseph. "We will have no more trouble with white people."

5. The Thief Treaty

However, the poles did not keep white people out of Wallowa Valley. Gold was found in nearby mountains, and miners poured into the valley. Troubles between red men and white became worse.

Joseph and Ollokot grew to be tall, handsome young men. Ollokot, gay and fun loving, was a fine athlete and an expert hunter. Sometimes he would go hunting for buffalo east of the Rocky Mountains. Joseph was more serious and thoughtful. Although he was a good hunter and a strong athlete, he did not often take part in sports. He spent much time with his father and learned to think like him.

The white man's law puzzled Joseph. If an Indian killed a settler or stole from him, the Indian was punished. But a white man could steal from an Indian or kill him, and nothing was done. There seemed to be one law for Indians and another for white men.

Joseph was bothered because the United States Government did not keep the promises Governor Stevens had made. No school was built on the Nez Perce reservation, and no money came for the Indians. It was said this was because the United States Senate had not ratified the treaty. Joseph could not understand this. White people seemed to have too many chiefs.

After four years the Senate finally ratified the treaty, and the government sent money to the tribes. But Tu-eka-kas would not take any.

"Never accept any presents from the government," the old chief told Joseph. "If you do, someday they will say you sold your land."

One sad day Joseph's older brother, Sousouquee, was accidentally killed. Tu-eka-kas grieved deeply for his oldest son, and Joseph's heart ached for him.

Lawyer
Hal-hal-tlos-tot
Head Chief of the Nez perce Tribe

Chief Lawyer was one of
the Nez Perce leaders who
were willing to sign away
the Wallowa Valley.

In 1863 the government called another Nez Perce
council to make a new treaty. Joseph, now 23, and
Ollokot took their feeble, ailing father to Lapwai.
The council was conducted by Indian commissioners
sent by the government.

"We cannot spare so much land for your tribe,"
they told the Nez Perces. "You must give up 10,000
square miles. The Lapwai area must do for all Nez
Perces."

Joseph was stunned. All of Wallowa would be
taken from his people!

"No!" cried Tu-eka-kas. "We will not give up the
land of our fathers."

"No!" shouted Chief Looking Glass and Chief White Bird.

"No!" cried Chief Too-hool-hool-zote and Chief Hush-hush-cute.

One of the commissioners turned to Chief Lawyer. "What do *you* say to this new treaty?" he asked.

Lawyer's land would not be affected by the new treaty.

"Yes," said Lawyer. "I accept the new treaty."

The commissioner said, "Lawyer speaks for all Nez Perces."

Joseph rose. "Wallowa has been the homeland of my people for centuries," he said. "Lawyer cannot sell what is not his."

Still the commissioners did not listen. They had Lawyer and some of his sub-chiefs make their marks on the treaty. "You must move to Lapwai," Tu-eka-kas was told. "You do not own the Wallowa Valley now."

"If we ever owned the land, we own it still," Joseph insisted.

"Lawyer sold the land," they answered.

"Suppose," said Joseph, "a white man comes to me and says, 'Joseph, I want to buy your horses.' I say, 'No, I will not sell them.'

"Then the white man goes to my neighbor and says, 'I want to buy Joseph's horses, but he will not sell.' My neighbor offers, 'Pay me the money, and I will sell you Joseph's horses.'

"The white man returns to me and says, 'Your neighbor sold me your horses.' Do you think I would give them up?"

The commissioners repeated, "Wallowa no longer belongs to you."

Old Tu-eka-kas shouted, "I tear up your thief treaty!" He tore the paper to bits. Then he took his precious Bible out of the folds of his blanket. With a mighty effort he tore it too.

"I tear up the white man's religion!" the old chief cried. "From where the sun now stands, I will have nothing that belongs to the white man!"

Tu-eka-kas stalked out of the council. Joseph, Ollokot, and all their people followed.

6. Chief Joseph

The Nez Perces were now like two separate tribes. Chief Lawyer's band and several others were called treaty Indians, because they had signed the "thief treaty." The rest were called nontreaty Indians, and they were considered to be troublemakers because they had refused to sign.

Joseph shared his father's fury and grief over the "thief treaty." But in his own life he had found great happiness. He had fallen in love with Springtime, a Nez Perce girl in Lawyer's band. Soon she became his wife.

Now Joseph and Springtime had a tepee of their own. Soon they had a little daughter, Sound-of-Running-Feet. About this time Ollokot married too. The brothers' lodges were close together.

Every day Joseph went to see his aged father. Tu-eka-kas was nearly blind now. When he rode his horse, a small boy sat in front of him. Day by day he became weaker. Now Joseph acted as chief in his father's place.

One day Tu-eka-kas sent for Joseph. When he entered the tepee, Joseph knew his father was dying.

"My son," said the old chief, "my body is going to see the Great Spirit."

Joseph bowed his head.

"When I am gone," the dying man went on, "think of your country. Never sell this land."

Joseph pressed his father's hand. "I will never sell it," Joseph promised. Chief Tu-eka-kas died peacefully. He was buried in beautiful Wallowa Valley.

Then the head men of the village met in council and elected Joseph as their chief. He was 31 years old.

Ollokot was glad and proud. "You will be a great chief, my brother," he said. "I will always help you."

Trouble with white men increased. Settlers tried to keep Nez Perces off their land. They stole Appaloosa horses and Nez Perce cattle. They accused Indians of stealing livestock. Indians who protested were killed. With great difficulty Joseph kept his young men from fighting back.

Time after time Joseph rode up to Lapwai and complained to the Indian agent, but nothing was done.

Sometimes the young braves accused Joseph of being a coward, but wise men knew it took more courage to endure insults than to fight back.

One autumn Joseph and his people went to Camas Meadows to gather their winter supply of camas roots. The young men rode ahead. Soon they returned, very angry.

"White settlers have ruined our camas crop!" they cried. "Their pigs have dug up the roots."

"Because the roots grow wild," said Joseph, "the white men think they are unimportant. Come, my people. We will find another camas field." He turned his horse around. The young braves grumbled, but they followed him.

Joseph tried to make the new settlers understand how the Indians felt. He tried without success to persuade them all to leave Wallowa. For years Joseph and his people suffered many, many wrongs.

Finally, Joseph rode to Lapwai again to see John Monteith, who was the new Indian agent.

"For many winters," Joseph said, "I have been talking to the white people. It is strange that they do not yet understand what I say. Let me go to Washington and talk to the president."

Mr. Monteith refused. However, he wrote to the president, and the president issued an order: "Wallowa Valley is not to be settled by white men. It is reserved for the Nez Perce Indians."

Joseph was happy.

Some of the settlers who streamed into Oregon in the late 1870s under the protection of troops

But white men protested that a valley the size of Massachusetts was too much to give to Indians. So the president changed his mind and opened Wallowa to settlers.

"The president speaks with a forked tongue," said Joseph bitterly.

7. Thirty Days To Move

Every year Mr. Monteith visited Chief Joseph. He brought presents and money. Each time he said, "You must move to the Lapwai Reservation."

Joseph was always courteous, but he accepted no presents or money. "We want nothing from the government," he said. "My people are satisfied here in Wallowa."

At last the government sent General Howard to Lapwai with an army. The general invited Joseph to a council. The other nontreaty Nez Perce chiefs went too.

"The United States Government orders you to move to the reservation," said the general.

Too-hool-hool-zote spoke hotly. "The Great Spirit made part of the world for us to live on. Where do you get the authority to say we should not live there?"

"I am the white war chief of this country,"

General Howard answered sharply. "Do you deny my authority? I will put you in jail!" And he did.

The young braves wanted revenge.

"No," said Joseph. "The arrest is wrong, but we must not break the peace."

The council went on for several days. Finally General Howard snapped, "Talk is useless. I must carry out my orders."

Joseph looked at Ollokot and the other chiefs. They all knew that they must move to the reservation or fight the United States Army.

"My people are like deer," Joseph said to the one-armed general. "Your people are like grizzly bears. We cannot hold our own against you. We will move to the reservation."

"You are wise, Joseph," said General Howard. "I will expect you here in 30 days with all your people."

"Why are you in such a hurry?" asked Joseph. "Thirty suns is not half enough time." He explained that their horses and cattle were scattered. The rivers were high with spring floods and would be dangerous to cross.

General Howard repeated stubbornly: "Thirty days is all you can have. My soldiers will come if you are late. Then you will lose your horses and cattle."

Finally Joseph agreed.

As the Indian Wars drew to a close, thousands of
Indians began to move sadly onto reservations.
Chief Joseph's Nez Perces were among them.

When he reached Wallowa, Joseph's daughter, Sound-of-Running-Feet, ran excitedly to meet him. "Soldiers are here!" she cried.

Joseph was angry. General Howard had not waited 30 days!

Joseph called a council. As he had expected, the young men wanted to fight. Older men were undecided.

Joseph advised against fighting. "Let us go to the reservation at once."

Sadly the people packed to leave their homeland. Men went to round up horses and cattle. Many animals had ranged too far to be rounded up and had to be left behind.

Out of Wallowa Valley rode the Nez Perce band —500 men, women, old people, and children. Packed on horses were all their belongings. The people were sad. Joseph's heart was heavy, too.

The Snake River was dangerously high. Women, children, and family treasures were placed on rafts. With a mounted warrior at each corner, the rafts were ferried across the river.

Then the men drove the livestock into the stream. Suddenly a fierce rainstorm came up, and many animals were swept far down the river. While the Indians worked to save them, white men came and stole many Appaloosa horses.

At last the Indians reached Rocky Canyon, just outside the boundary line of the reservation. The other nontreaty bands were assembled there. A grand council was held, and there was much war talk. Joseph had great difficulty in getting the council to agree to peace.

When he thought the danger of war was over, Joseph went to butcher some beef for his family. As he was returning he heard dreadful news. White Bird's young braves had killed four white men.

Sadly Joseph followed as the other Indians rode to White Bird Canyon. War was unavoidable now.

8. War!

At dawn soldiers came riding down into White Bird Canyon. Joseph sent six warriors with a white truce flag to meet them. But soldiers fired on the flag of truce, and the battle began.

There were only 60 Indian fighters, and few had guns, but it seemed as if there were hundreds. Their heads bobbed up from rocks or brush to fire, then they dropped out of sight. A herd of horses galloped through the army's lines, with Indians hanging from the horses' sides and shooting from under their necks. The soldiers retreated.

Because Joseph had been the spokesman for the

Looking Glass was elected as war chief of the nontreaty Nez Perces on the terrible journey across Idaho.

nontreaty Indians for years, General Howard held him responsible for the fighting. He sent word that if Joseph surrendered, the other Indians could go free. But Joseph knew that the white men had never kept their word to the Indians, so he would not surrender.

The Indians elected Looking Glass as war chief. Joseph was chosen guardian of the families, because all the people trusted him. And the Nez Perces started east across the Bitterroot Mountains on the Lolo Trail, a steep, dangerous trail 250 miles long.

When they had almost finished their terrible eleven-day journey across Idaho, scouts brought bad news.

"A fort has been built across Lolo Trail," the scouts said. "Captain Rawn's soldiers threaten to keep us out of Montana."

The chiefs went to the fort to talk to Captain Rawn.

"We wish to go through this country," said Looking Glass.

"We come in peace," said Joseph.

"You may pass," Captain Rawn answered, "if you give me your guns, ammunition, and horses."

"No," replied Joseph. "Without horses, our families cannot travel. Without guns, we would be at the mercy of any soldier we meet."

"Then you cannot pass," replied the captain.

The chiefs returned to their people. Joseph sent young men to find a way out of the canyon, and they cleared another trail. It was hidden from the fort and out of rifle range.

The next morning a few warriors began to fire on the fort. While the soldiers were busy firing back, Joseph took the families and baggage over the new trail.

Now that they were in Montana, the Nez Perces thought they were safe.

"We left the war and General Howard in Idaho," said Joseph.

On August 7 the Indians camped in Big Hole Basin. Looking Glass, their war chief, would not post sentries.

Under Joseph's direction, the people cut lodge poles, caught fish, and shot game. For two days everybody worked.

Before dawn the third day, General Gibbon, who was in charge of that area, found the sleeping camp. Soldiers fired into tepees and killed women, children, and warriors. Springtime, Joseph's wife, and Fair Land, Ollokot's wife, were wounded. Fair Land died soon after.

When the soldiers retreated to the bluffs above the camp, Joseph gathered the women, children, old people, and the injured. He led them away, while warriors fought off the soldiers.

On went the fleeing Indians, and the soldiers followed them. General Howard caught up with General Gibbon, and they both pursued Chief Joseph.

One day Looking Glass protested, "Why do we hurry? Our people are tired, and our horses lame."

"We must reach Canada," Joseph said.

"The one-armed general is four suns behind us," said Looking Glass. "We can travel more slowly."

The other chiefs agreed, and Joseph said no more.

On September 29 the Indians camped at the foot of Bearpaw Mountain, only a few miles from Canada and freedom. The next morning a new army under Colonel Miles found them!

Joseph was with the horse herd, away from the lodges, helping families pack their belongings. Suddenly he saw some soldiers riding down the hill.

"Hurry!" he shouted to his daughter, helping her onto a horse. "Ride north! Find Sitting Bull in Canada. Ask him to send warriors!"

Sound-of-Running-Feet rode quickly away as did all the women and children who were ready. But many of them could not leave, for soldiers surrounded the camp.

Joseph was cut off from the camp. Unarmed, he dashed through their lines. His horse was wounded, and his clothes were bullet-riddled.

His wife met him at the door of their lodge. "Here is your gun!" she cried.

The Indians soon drove the soldiers back up the hill. But many brave Nez Perces had been killed, including Ollokot and Too-hool-hool-zote.

Colonel Miles stationed many soldiers around the camp. No one was allowed in or out. Joseph knew that the colonel hoped to starve his people into surrender.

9. "I Will Fight No More Forever"

For Joseph, the night that followed was the blackest of his life. His brother Ollokot was dead. He did not know what would happen to his people —those who had escaped, and those who remained.

During that night the women dug trenches with frying pans and camas sticks. Dried meat was fed to the children. Grownups went hungry.

There were no fires. The wind was thick with snow. Children cried. Old people suffered in silence. It was a fearful night.

When morning came, the battle was resumed. The Indians fought from the gullies and trenches.

"Save your ammunition," Joseph told the men. "Fire at the voice that gives a command." Many officers were killed in the battle.

That afternoon Colonel Miles raised a white flag. He asked to talk to Joseph.

"Do not go," Looking Glass urged. "Whites cannot be trusted."

But Joseph went to meet the colonel.

"If your people surrender all guns," Colonel Miles said, "we will stop the war."

"Let us keep half our rifles," Joseph requested. "We need them to shoot game."

The colonel refused. Joseph started back down the

hill, but soldiers grabbed him. Looking Glass was right, Joseph thought. This was the second truce white soldiers had broken. Joseph was rolled in a blanket and put in a tent with mules.

Next morning Yellow Bull came to Colonel Miles's camp with a white flag.

"One of your officers is our prisoner," he said. "Release Chief Joseph, or we will kill him."

Colonel Miles released Joseph, and the battle went on.

On the third day Joseph saw many dark objects moving through the snow.

"Sitting Bull!" he exclaimed. "He has come to our rescue!"

His people laughed and shouted in wild relief. Then, as the figures came closer, joy turned to despair. It was only a herd of buffalo!

On the fifth day army scouts again approached the Indian camp with a flag of truce. They brought new surrender terms. The people would be given food and blankets. In the spring they would be sent to the reservation.

Joseph's heart ached for his people. They had lost everything they owned—land, horses, cattle, money. In eleven weeks they had traveled 1,700 miles. They had fought twelve battles without surrendering. But this time, no victory was possible.

The surrender of Chief Joseph, October 4, 1877

"I am going to surrender," Joseph said to his warriors. "It is for the starving, freezing families. For myself I do not care."

White Bird and Looking Glass would not surrender. They planned to escape to Canada. White Bird and some of his band got away, but Looking Glass was killed by a sniper's bullet.

At four o'clock on the raw, windy afternoon of October 4, 1877, Chief Joseph rode up the hill. Hush-hush-cute and five other warriors went with him. Colonel Miles waited at the half-way mark. General Howard was with him.

Joseph swung off his horse. He handed his rifle to an officer and began to speak:

Tell General Howard I know his heart. . . . I am tired of fighting. Our chiefs are killed. . . . Looking Glass is dead. He who led the young men is dead. It is cold and we have no blankets. The little children are freezing to death. . . . Hear me, my chiefs. I am tired. My heart is sick and sad. From where the sun now stands, I will fight no more forever.

Then the remaining Nez Perces came up the hill. They gave up their rifles, their horses, and saddles. More than 400 Nez Perces surrendered, including 147 children.

The United States Government did not keep Colonel Miles's promises to Joseph. The Indians were sent to Bismarck, North Dakota; to Leavenworth, Kansas; and finally to Indian Territory. Many died in these strange surroundings.

Eight long years passed before the destitute Nez Perces were returned to the Northwest. Only 269 remained. Idaho settlers refused to accept Joseph, so his people were sent to Colville Reservation in the state of Washington. There Joseph died, on September 21, 1904.

Gradually Americans realized that Chief Joseph was a great man, a great leader, and a great humanitarian. Many tributes were paid to his memory. A fine monument was erected, and towns, streets, schools, and a ship were named for him. Finally, in June 1956, Chief Joseph Dam on the Columbia River was dedicated.

Probably Chief Joseph would have preferred another kind of tribute. He would have liked Americans to stop mistreating people of his or any other race. For once he said:

> If the white man wants to live in peace with the Indian . . . there need be no trouble. Treat all men alike. Give them all the same laws. Give them all an even chance to live and grow. All men were made by the same Great Spirit. They are brothers.

In the Words of Chief Joseph

"The White men were many and we could not hold our own with them. We were like deer. They were like grizzly bears. We had a small country. Their country was large. We were contented to let things remain as the Great Spirit made them. They were not, and would change the rivers if they did not suit them."

"The earth was created by the assistance of the sun and it should be left as it was. . . . The country was made without lines of demarcation, and it is no man's business to divide it. . . . Do not misunderstand me, but understand me fully with reference to my affection for the land. I never said the land was mine to do with it as I chose. The one who has the right to dispose of it is the one who has created it. I claim a right to live on my land, and accord you the privilege to live on yours."

About Chief Joseph's People

The Nez Perces lived in the basin area of the Snake and Columbia Rivers in what is today Idaho, Oregon, and Washington. The Nez Perce nation was divided into bands on a geographical basis. Each village had its own chief, fishing place, and strip of territory along the river. Since the Nez Perces did not grow their own crops, they depended mainly on wild plants—particularly the camas root—game, and fish for their food supply. Mounted on their beautiful Appaloosa horses, many of them ventured onto the Great Plains to hunt buffalo. The map below shows where Joseph's people lived and the route they followed in their last bid for freedom.

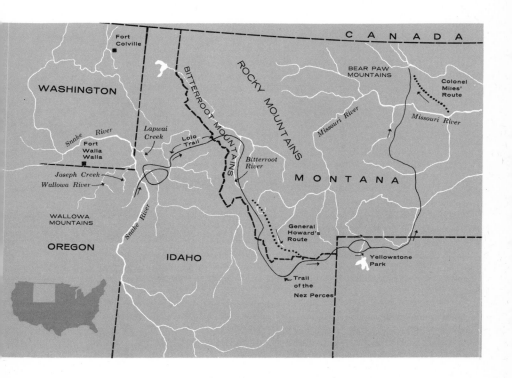

Index

G

Gall, Chief, 29
Ghost Dance religion, 45, 46–47 (pic)
Gibbon, John, 153
Gold, 33, 38, 71, 138
Good-Voiced-Elk, 17, 18
Grand River, 25, 28, 45
Guardian Spirit dance, 134

H

High Buffalo, 115
Horseback, Chief, 99–100
Howard, Oliver, 146–147, 149, 151, 153
Hump (brother of Crazy Horse), 54, 58, 59, 60, 63, 65, 66, 68
Hunkpaca Sioux, 13, 16, 17, 20, 21, 24, 25, 31, 42
Hush-hush-cute, 141, 157

I

Indians
Apache, 103–104
Arapaho, 35, 104
Assiniboine, 20, 21, 31–32
Blackfoot, 35
Brulé Sioux, 25, 62, 63, 65
Cheyenne, 35, 68, 104
Comanche, 90, 91, 96, 97, 100 (pic)
Crow, 17, 18, 19
Hunkpapa Sioux, 13, 17, 20, 21, 24, 25, 31, 42
Kiowa, 104
Miniconjou Sioux, 35
Nez Perce, 127, 128, 130–131, 135, 136, 137, 140, 144, 145, 148 (pic), 158
Oglala Sioux, 25, 35, 38, 54, 57, 61, 65, 74, 83
Quahada Comanche, 101, 106, 115, 116
Sioux, 10, 13, 14 (pic), 15, 18 (pic), 19, 25, 45, 61, 77–78

Isa-tai, medicine man, 108, 109, 110, 114

J

Joseph, Chief
at Big Hole Basin, 153
becomes chief, 143
childhood of, 126, 127, 128, 129, 130, 131–133
death of, 159
and death of father, 143
education of, 126, 127
as guardian of the families, 151
keeps vigil, 132–133
at Lapwai council meeting, 140, 141
tries to move tribe to Lapwai reservation, 149
leads tribe over Lolo Trail, 151–152
marriage of, 142–143
as peaceful mediator, 144–145, 147, 149
and Sitting Bull, 154, 156
surrenders to General Howe, 157 (pic), 158
becomes Thunder-Rolling-in-the-Mountains, 134
at Walla Walla council meeting, 135, 137, 138
Jumping Bull (father of Sitting Bull), 13, 15, 16, 17, 18, 19

K

Kicking Bird, 104
Kills-Often, 22, 31, 32, 48, 49
Kiowa Indians, 104

L

Lapwai Reservation, 146
Lawyer, Chief, 140 (pic), 141, 142
Lewis and Clark expedition, 130
Little Bighorn, Battle of, 37–38, 79, 80–81 (pic), 82